# Faculty Success in the Academy

# Research, Theory, and Practice Within Academic Affairs

Series Editors
Antione D. Tomlin and Sherella Cupid

The mission of the *Research, Theory, and Practice Within Academic Affairs* series seeks to explore current trends, practices, and challenges within academic affairs.

This book series will include a plethora of topics with particular attention to the personal and live experiences of individuals who work in higher education academic affairs spaces in various colleges and universities. The intended audience is academic affairs administrators, leaders, educators, policymakers, researchers, and others interested in learning more about the experiences of academic affairs professionals.

## OTHER TITLES IN THE SERIES

Escape the Cape, From Existing to Evolving: Amplifying Voices of Black and Brown Women in the Mental Health Profession

Innovative Approaches, Practices, and Strategies in Adult Education

The Journey: Truths of Same-Gender-Loving Black Males in Higher Education

# Faculty Success in the Academy

## Tips, Tools, and Resources for Success

*Edited by*

## Antione D. Tomlin
**Anne Arundel Community College, USA**

*And*

## Hiawatha Smith
**University of Wisconsin-River Falls, USA**

United Kingdom – North America – Japan
India – Malaysia – China

Emerald Publishing Limited
Emerald Publishing, Floor 5, Northspring, 21-23 Wellington Street, Leeds LS1 4DL

First edition 2026

Copyright © 2026 by Emerald Publishing Limited.
All rights of reproduction in any form reserved.

Cover photo: iStock and Hispanolistic

**Reprints and permissions service**
Contact: www.copyright.com

No part of this book may be reproduced, stored in a retrieval system, transmitted in any form or by any means electronic, mechanical, photocopying, recording or otherwise without either the prior written permission of the publisher or a licence permitting restricted copying issued in the UK by The Copyright Licensing Agency and in the USA by The Copyright Clearance Center. Any opinions expressed in the chapters are those of the authors. Whilst Emerald makes every effort to ensure the quality and accuracy of its content, Emerald makes no representation implied or otherwise, as to the chapters' suitability and application and disclaims any warranties, express or implied, to their use.

**British Library Cataloguing in Publication Data**
A catalogue record for this book is available from the British Library

ISBN: 978-1-80592-288-9 (Print hardback)
ISBN: 978-1-80592-290-2 (Print paperback)
ISBN: 978-1-80592-287-2 (Ebook)
ISBN: 978-1-80592-289-6 (Epub)

Typeset by TNQ Tech
Cover design by TNQ Tech

# CONTENTS

About the Editors ................................................................... vii

About the Contributors ............................................................. ix

Navigating Academia: Illuminating Pathways to Faculty
Success ..................................................................................... 1
*McKenzie Rabenn*

## SECTION 1

### IT'S NOT JUST WHAT YOU KNOW, BUT WHO YOU KNOW AND ARE CONNECTED TO

1   The Architect and the Motherscholar: Lessons in the Elusive
Art of Networking in the Academy ......................................... 9
*Tierney B. Hinman*

2   Building Intentional Community and Support ..................... 21
*Kimberly M. Baker*

3   Faculty Success: A Path Worth Traveling ............................. 29
*Mary E. Robinson*

4   This What Got Me Thru": Black Mothering, Othermothering,
and Furthermothering in Academia ...................................... 37
*Amir Asim Gilmore*

5   At Your Service: Building Community and Professional
Identity Through Service ....................................................... 51
*Anne K. Weed*

## SECTION 2

### I CAN'T DO THIS ON MY OWN, YOU CAN'T EITHER

6. Experiences and Mentoring Needs of a New International Counselor Educator in the US ............ 65
   *Suelle Micallef Marmara*

7. A Bit of Advice for Early Career Faculty ............ 75
   *Karen R. Tellez-Chaires*

8. Bridging the Gap in Higher Education: Inspiring Journeys of Women of Color in Early Childhood Education ............ 83
   *Sabrina F. Hinton, Saleena Frazier and Raleta Dawkins*

9. Successful Teaching in Higher Education: How Experience as a Public-School Teacher, Outdoor Educator, and School Counselor Helped Set the Stage for Teaching Success ............ 91
   *Mark C. Gillen*

## SECTION 3

### LEARN THE SYSTEM, BEAT THE SYSTEM

10. Success in Higher Education: Practical Tips From a Long-Time Professor ............ 101
    *Stephan E. Sargent*

11. The Intersection of Finesse and Strategy: Navigating the Academy as a Faculty of Color ............ 109
    *Kevin L. Wright*

12. My Journey From "Nothing" to Receiving an Outstanding Faculty Award in a Dozen Years ............ 117
    *David L. Largent*

13. Metamorphosis of Young Faculty: Navigating Academic Selfhood in Higher Education ............ 125
    *Christopher A. Hinton*

14. The Illusive Rank and Promotion Journey ............ 133
    *Latonia V. Moss*

# ABOUT THE EDITORS

**Antione D. Tomlin, PhD**: Rooted in core values like Autonomy, Flexibility, Learning, Respect, Transparency, Honesty, and Fun, I live and breathe principles that not only shape my life but also guide my interactions with others. As a proud native of Baltimore City, these values have been my compass in navigating life's journey. Being a first-generation undergrad and grad student, I recognize the transformative power of education, a value intricately tied to my passion for continuous learning. This passion steered me into a fulfilling career in higher education, where I've been teaching English since 2013. The classroom, for me, is an ever-inspiring space filled with dedicated students who continually fuel my curiosity and growth. Beyond teaching, I wear the hat of a trained and certified Life and Engagement Coach, proudly holding the Professional Certified Coach (PCC) credential from the International Coach Federation (ICF). Feel free to explore more about my coaching venture, Best AT Coaching!, LLC. As a Baltimore native, I earned my academic stripes from local institutions: a BS in psychology from Stevenson University, an MA in higher education administration and student affairs from Morgan State University, and a PhD in language, literacy, and culture from the University of Maryland, Baltimore County. My current research focuses on the experiences of Black and Brown faculty, staff, and students in higher education.

**Hiawatha Smith, PhD,** is an Associate Professor of literacy education at the University of Wisconsin-River Falls. There, he primarily teaches graduate and undergraduate courses in *children's and adolescent literature* as well as *English language arts methods*. In addition to his teaching responsibilities, he is the director of the graduate reading education and elementary education programs while also supervising preservice teachers. Hiawatha, a native North Carolinian, attended North Carolina Agricultural and Technical State University, where he earned his undergraduate and graduate degrees in Elementary Education. He earned his PhD at the University of

North Carolina Greensboro in Educational Studies with an emphasis in Literacy Education. Prior to his time in higher education, Hiawatha was a classroom teacher at multiple grade levels as well as a curriculum facilitator. Hiawatha's scholarly activities include research, publications, and presentations crossing multiple areas of literacy (and teacher education), including preservice teachers in practicum experiences, reading motivation, nonproficient readers, developmental word study instruction, and diverse perspectives in children's and adolescent literature. He is a member of the Diversity Scholars Network at the University of Michigan, a 2022 NCTE Early Career Educator of Color award recipient, and has membership in various professional literacy-related organizations.

# ABOUT THE CONTRIBUTORS

**Kimberly M. Baker, PhD,** is an Associate Professor in the Department of Sociology, Criminology, and Anthropology at the University of Northern Iowa. As a sociologist, her research focuses on the social control of substance use. More recently, she has conducted interviews on students navigating higher education, including students working full time while attending school and students' requests for extensions and excused absences.

**Raleta Dawkins** is an educator who is a true life-long learner. She brings experience teaching in both elementary and collegiate settings. She enjoys engaging and working with young scholars using authentic learning opportunities that impact their desire to grow and innovate. Dr Dawkins is a proud alumnus of North Carolina Agricultural and Technical State University (BS and MA in elementary education) and Old Dominion University (PhD).

**Saleena Frazier** is a childcare entrepreneur in Winston-Salem, North Carolina. Frazier holds a bachelor's degree in business administration and a master's in information and technology management from the University of North Carolina at Greensboro. In 2019, she received a Doctorate in Organizational Leadership with an emphasis on Organizational Development. She began her career within the banking industry in Charlotte, North Carolina in 1996 and since has worked dually as an Adjunct for various institutions of higher learning. Dr Fraziers goal is to meet the needs of the growing community and to maintain standards of quality in educating children while understanding the significance that early childhood education has on the future achievements of children, both in school and in life. She is excited to offer a highly individualized preschool program in the Forsyth County community and is looking forward to making a positive impact through research and voluntarism.

**Mark C. Gillen** started his career as a fifth-grade teacher. He also taught middle school English and Math, as well as running outdoor training trips, working in a day treatment program and for the last 20 years as a faculty member in the Counseling and School Psychology Department at the University of Wisconsin-River Falls.

**Amir Asim Gilmore, PhD,** is an Associate Professor in Cultural Studies and Social Thought in Education at Washington State University. His interdisciplinary background in Cultural Studies, Africana Studies, and Education allows him to traverse the boundaries across the social sciences, the arts, and the humanities. Amir's broad research interests are Black Aesthetics, Black Masculinities, Afrofuturism, Afro-Pessimism, and the political economy of schooling.

**Tierney B. Hinman, PhD,** is currently an Assistant Professor of Literacy Education with the Department of Curriculum and Teaching at Auburn University. Her research focuses on culturally and linguistically responsive literacy instruction in the content areas, including supporting teachers in critically implementing disciplinary literacy in ways that value and leverage students' family, community, and cultural knowledge in the sensemaking process. To interrogate and take action for change in her own teaching practice, Dr Hinman also participates in a long-term self-study community of practice centered on equity and social justice in teacher preparation. Dr Hinman identifies as a motherscholar with three young children who are often, in one form or another, research and teaching/learning partners.

**Christopher A. Hinton, PhD, MBA,** dynamic scholar-practitioner whose career spans higher education, organizational leadership, and community impact. He currently serves as Vice President of Institutional Advancement at Barber-Scotia College, Project Manager for Campus Life at Winston-Salem State University, and Chief Operating Officer of the Academy Network of Winston-Salem, overseeing a network of early learning centers. With a PhD in Global Leadership from Indiana Institute of Technology, an MBA in Human Resource Management from North Carolina A&T State University, and dual undergraduate degrees from Appalachian State University, Dr. Hinton's academic background reflects a deep commitment to lifelong learning and equity-centered leadership. His research centers the lived experiences of Generation Z Black professionals in Historically Black Colleges and Universities (HBCU) student affairs leadership. An accomplished educator, he has taught business and management courses at High Point University, North Carolina A&T, and beyond—integrating innovation, inclusion, and critical thinking into every learning space. His leadership extends beyond the classroom through board service with the YMCA of Northwest North Carolina, the Child Care Resource Center, and Delta Fine Arts Center. A celebrated leader, Dr. Hinton has been recognized with the Human Relations Award from the City of Winston-Salem, the 40 Under 40 Most Influential African Americans in the Triad, and HBCU Buzz's 30 Under 30. He is a member of Sigma Alpha Pi, Omicron Delta Kappa, Sigma Iota Epsilon, and a distinguished Alain Leroy Locke inductee of Phi Beta Sigma Fraternity, Inc. His work bridges education, advocacy, and innovation—transforming institutions and empowering communities.

**Sabrina F. Hinton** is an entrepreneur, early childhood specialist, licensed teacher, childcare advocate, motivational coach, and educational trainer who is a highly regarded administrator in the private and public preschool sector. Hinton is the recipient of multiple professional and community awards which include the prestigious Outstanding Leadership and Service to our Community Award from the city of Winston-Salem and The Winston-Salem Mayor's Council for Persons with Disabilities Citizen Involvement Award. Currently, Hinton is engaged in research and service that impacts the quality of life of the citizens of Forsyth County at the local, state, and national levels. She works closely with educators, students, families, and children to build a greater framework of quality in the early childhood arena. Hinton quotes "I am committed to cultivating a vibrant and engaged community in Forsyth County and beyond. And I pray my impact is felt throughout the world."

**David L. Largent, MS,** is a Senior Lecturer in the Department of Computer Science at Ball State University in Muncie, Indiana, USA. Dave enjoys being part of other's learning, and especially likes seeing a "light bulb" turn on when something suddenly "clicks" for a learner. He was awarded the 2022 Outstanding Faculty Award, BSU's highest faculty award. This earned him the responsibility of delivering the summer 2023 BSU commencement address! Dave occasionally dabbles in research focusing on pedagogy, alternative assessment, and diversity, equity, and inclusion. University teaching is a second career for him, having worked in industry as a computer programmer and department manager, after earning a BS in social work and an A.A. in computer applications from Manchester University. He left industry after nearly three decades, earned a master's degree, and has been teaching for over a decade since then.

**Suelle Micallef Marmara', PhD,** is an Assistant Professor in Counseling at the Hofstra University in New York. She earned a PhD in Counseling Education and Supervision from Old Dominion University and a dual Master's in Transcultural Counseling from the University of Maryland College Park and the University of Malta. She worked with hospitalized patients, persons experiencing domestic violence, immigration, and prisoners following drug rehabilitation programs. She established the counseling services of a new infertility clinic at Malta's General Hospital and directed the counseling services in seven different government schools in Malta. She served as a council member on the counseling council, which regulates

Malta's counseling profession. Dr Micallef Marmara' has a research background in transcultural issues, clinical supervision, and counseling in hospital settings. She delivered several presentations, published research on healthcare professionals' perspectives on mental health counselors' tasks in hospital settings, and co-authored a book chapter on counselors as agents of social justice.

**Latonia V. Moss, EdD, MFA,** is a renowned educator and motivational speaker with over two decades of experience in higher education. She advocates for educational reform, emphasizing the importance of instilling soft skills in students to foster confidence and character. Dr Moss is a passionate advocate for diversity, equity, and inclusion in academia, addressing racial inequities within curricula. As a representative for Black students, she shares her own journey, highlighting education's transformative power in shifting her from delinquency to purposeful upward mobility. Dr Moss has contributed to various publications: Exploring DEIA: Outside and Inside the Margins, The Prophesied Place: Navigating a Career in Higher Education and Supporting Students of Color in Language Learning Environments. Beyond academia, she is a playwright, poet, and is currently working on her debut novel, *Mind the Glass*. Dr Moss is a dynamic force for positive change, using her diverse talents to impact education and beyond.

**McKenzie Rabenn, PhD,** a resident of Eagle River, Wisconsin, shares her passion for education as an Adjunct Professor in literacy education at both UW-River Falls and UW-Superior. Additionally, she serves as a professional development facilitator for the University of North Dakota. Her extensive career in elementary education spans across the Midwest, culminating in the attainment of a PhD in Teaching and Learning from the University of North Dakota (UND). Driven by a fervor for enhancing educational practices, Dr Rabenn's research interests revolve around online learning, teacher professional development, literacy, and rural education. Through her scholarly endeavors and unwavering commitment to teaching, she endeavors to bring about positive transformations in the lives of both educators and students. Her dedication to fostering impactful educational experiences stands at the forefront of her endeavors.

**Mary E. Robinson** has over 20 years of experience as an Educator. She is an English and Reading Professor/IERW Coordinator at Montgomery College in Maryland who teaches face-to-face or distance learning courses. As a proponent of the value of professional development, she is the recipient of Open Education Resource and MOST Fellowships. Mary is the Membership Chairperson for NOSS MD and has earned—micro-credential badges for OERs, Hypothesis AI, and Quality Assurance. In addition, Mary is a QM Peer Reviewer, content expert, and/or dissertation Chair for GCU and other graduate students seeking to attain their doctoral degrees. Mary has peer-reviewed AERA and the Journal of Interdisciplinary Studies in Education articles or proposals. Professor Robinson is the MC 2020–2021 Faculty of the Year. Mary is a lifelong learner and enjoys teaching and advising students to attain their academic goals. In her spare time, Mary enjoys swimming and bowling.

**Stephan E. Sargent, EdD,** after graduating from Oklahoma State University with a bachelor's in education, Dr Sargent taught elementary school in Ponca City, Oklahoma. Dr Sargent graduated from The University of Tulsa with a master's in school counseling and Oklahoma State University with a doctorate in reading/literacy. Dr Sargent has also taught developmental reading to adults, reading methods courses, and study skills courses. Later, he began work at Northeastern State University (NSU) in Oklahoma as a professor of reading methods. He teaches graduate and undergraduate courses in reading methods and works extensively in the NSU Reading Clinic. Dr Sargent works closely with area schools, teaching the majority of his courses in clinical settings. Additionally, Dr Sargent works closely with school accreditation at all levels. He received the Cognia Excellence in Education Award for Oklahoma.

**Karen R. Tellez-Chaires, PhD,** is an Assistant Professor at Cal Poly Pomona in the Department of English and Modern Languages. Her educational background and research interests are in border, feminist, and cultural rhetorics. She is a Graduate Assistant advisor for Rhetoric and Composition and works with undergraduate students as a mentor for The Research through Inclusive Opportunities (RIO) program. Her work has appeared in the interdisciplinary journal *Writers, Craft, and Context*, and has a forthcoming chapter in the edited collection, *Revising Moves*. Karen is also the recipient of the 2022–2023 NCTE Early Career Educator of Color Leadership Award.

**Anne K. Weed, PhD,** began her career as an adjunct teaching composition for Keuka College before joining the faculty full time in 1997. She is emerita professor of English at Keuka College where she has held numerous leadership roles. She has chaired the Humanities and Fine Arts Division and served as Interim Associate Provost and Vice President for Academic Affairs. Additionally, she has served as a peer reviewer and visiting accreditation team member for the Middle States Commission on Higher Education. She was named Keuka College's 2007 Professor of the Year. Anne holds a PhD in English from the University of Rochester and has a BA in English and French from Goucher College. She lives in the Finger Lakes Region of New York.

**Kevin L. Wright, EdD**, a proud native of Las Vegas' Historic Westside and descendant of African, Creole, and Indigenous ancestry, serves as a faculty member at Southern New Hampshire University. He specializes in raising consciousness, building equity-centered skills, and developing strategies to shift organizational cultures and systems. His work is rooted in a deep commitment to racial justice and advocacy for historically marginalized communities. Kevin holds a bachelor's in Business Communications from Northern Arizona University, a master's in Student Affairs Administration from Lewis & Clark College, and a doctorate in Organizational Leadership from Northcentral University.

# NAVIGATING ACADEMIA: ILLUMINATING PATHWAYS TO FACULTY SUCCESS

**McKenzie Rabenn**
*University of Wisconsin-River Falls, USA*
*University of North Dakota*

As we embark on our journey through academia, we often find ourselves navigating uncharted waters, seeking guidance, inspiration, and, above all, a sense of belonging in this diverse and dynamic landscape of higher education. It is a journey filled with opportunities and challenges, where the quest for success is met with myriad experiences, both enriching and demanding.

The experiences of first-year, tenure track faculty have been missing in the literature about new or junior faculty for many years (Cole et al., 2017). I find myself in a unique position as I pen these words, just one year removed from the completion of my own PhD, navigating the labyrinthine halls of academia. It's a journey that I continue to embark upon, with every day presenting new opportunities for growth and learning. This journey, while often viewed as idyllic from outside the academy, poses significant challenges, particularly for newcomers. As research has demonstrated (e.g., Austin et al., 2007), new faculty members are typically highly committed and enthusiastic about their choice of career. However, they often encounter negative emotions and obstacles early on that can temper their idealism and reduce their effectiveness (Fayne & Ortquist-Ahrens, 2006). For many, the entry period, lasting from one term to several years, is marked by anxiety, pressure, and stress stemming from ambiguous expectations, a sense of isolation, and a lack of balance between personal and professional life. "Faculty Success in the Academy: Tips, Tools, and Resources for Success" is a beacon of wisdom and support for those who embark on this academic odyssey, including those, like me, who are just beginning to find their way.

Within the forthcoming pages, you will uncover a wealth of knowledge, heartfelt advice, and inspiring anecdotes shared by faculty members representing the full spectrum of higher education. It transcends the boundaries of public and private institutions, encompassing research-intensive universities and teaching-focused colleges, both predominantly white institutions (PWIs) and Minority Serving Institutions (MSIs). This book illuminates the journey from instructors to assistant professors and revered emeriti professors, serving as a wellspring of motivation and a trove of insights that intricately weave the tapestry of higher education, catering to the needs of both new and seasoned faculty members.

This book embraces a diverse academic community, resonating with the experiences of individuals from both historically majority and marginalized groups. Specifically, for faculty of color, who research has shown face racism, tokenism, and hostile campus environments (Jayakumar et al., 2009; Stanley, 2006), this can result in negative experiences including isolation, questioning of qualifications from students, invalidation of research from colleagues, and disproportionately high expectations of service (Diggs et al., 2009; Stanley, 2006; Tomlin, 2023; Tuitt et al., 2009). This guide serves as a beacon for all who have chosen the academic path, from those early in their career to those who are well into their careers. It has the potential to help each to better navigate their journey, embrace their unique identities, and thrive in the diverse realm of higher education across varied settings.

"Faculty Success in the Academy" is a testament to the power of mentorship, guidance, and shared experiences. It underscores the importance of building bridges, forming connections, and fostering a sense of belonging for all who aspire to thrive in the academic sphere. It provides invaluable tools and resources, coupled with stories of resilience, perseverance, and achievements, which will inspire and empower the next generation of academics, including those like me, who are one year removed from the halls of academia.

This comprehensive guide offers invaluable insights, strategies, and personal narratives from a diverse group of faculty members, illuminating the path to success within the academic world. Success in the academy can look different for different people, but many of the elements to success are found within this book. The book is divided into three essential sections, each focusing on a critical aspect of faculty life: mentorship, navigating academia, and networking.

## SECTION 1: NETWORKING

*It's not just what you know, but who you know and are connected to*

In this section, readers will explore the significance of networking within academia. Discover how individual, unique identities can be leveraged to navigate academic institutions that prioritize productivity. The chapters in this section redefine networking to include not only traditional definitions of productivity but also the overall well-being of individual members in the network. Learn from personal experiences and be inspired to re-imagine your own supportive academic network.

## SECTION 2: MENTORSHIP

*I can't do this on my own, you can't either*

In this section, readers will discover the profound impact of mentorship on faculty members' careers. Personal narratives provide readers with valuable lessons on how to navigate academia in a way that nurtures personal and professional growth. In this section, readers will learn how mentorship can help overcome challenges, gain recognition, and ultimately, contribute to the broader academic community.

## SECTION 3: NAVIGATING ACADEMIA

*Learn the system, beat the system*

In this section, readers will navigate the essentials within the complex landscape of academia as faculty members share their transformative journeys. From early challenges to emerging recognition, these narratives delve into the intricate tapestry of academia, uncovering strategies for success. Anchored in transformational leadership theory, this section offers insights and guidance for those embarking on similar trajectories.

This volume is more than just a guide; it's a call to action, reminding us that each of us brings a unique perspective and voice to the academy. It celebrates the remarkable contributions faculty members make daily to higher education and the broader community. It recognizes that the path to success is not a solitary one but a shared voyage filled with hidden opportunities for those who dare to explore.

"Faculty Success in the Academy" is a guiding light for those seeking to thrive in the vibrant tapestry of academia. Whether you're a new faculty member in need of guidance, a seasoned educator in search of new perspectives, or an academic leader dedicated to supporting your colleagues, this book offers valuable insights, encouragement, and a supportive community to help you excel in the diverse world of academia.

It's a collaborative effort that provides a community of wisdom, a shared journey, and a call to action for all faculty members, regardless of their career stage. With gratitude to the authors, editors, and contributors who have shared their wisdom, experiences, and stories, we invite you to embark on this transformative journey through the pages of this book. May it inspire, guide, and empower you to reach new heights of success in your academic endeavors.

As you embark on this enriching journey through the pages of this book, I encourage you to immerse yourself fully in its contents. Take a moment to contemplate your academic positionality and note areas where growth and improvement are beneficial for your success. Delve into the table of contents and author bios, identifying chapters and contributors that directly resonate with your immediate needs and aspirations. Remember, each chapter within these pages offers a unique opportunity for growth, regardless of your career stage. Embrace this diversity of perspectives and knowledge, allowing each word to enrich your understanding and propel you forward on your academic path. May this book be not just a source of information, but a catalyst for your personal and professional development.

More specifically, I suggest the following:

- Reflect on your current positionality as an academic. In what areas are you currently shining? In what areas do you feel you need a jumpstart?
- Explore the table of contents and author bios. Identify those that might provide an immediate need for your success.
- Read through all of the chapters, while the author might be at a different stage in their career, there is a space for growth through their experiences.
- Make a running list of ideas and strategies that you can immediately implement as well as those that you can work toward in the near future.

## REFERENCES

Austin, A. E., Sorcinelli, M. D., & McDaniels, M. (2007). Understanding new faculty background, aspirations, challenges, and growth. In *The scholarship of teaching and learning in higher education: An evidence-based perspective* (pp. 39–89). Springer.

Cole, E. R., McGowan, B. L., & Zerquera, D. D. (2017). First-year faculty of color: Narratives about entering the academy. *Equity & Excellence in Education, 50*(1), 1–12.

Diggs, G. A., Garrison-Wade, D. F., Estrada, D., & Galindo, R. (2009). Smiling faces and colored spaces: The experiences of faculty of color pursuing tenure in the academy. *Urban Review, 41,* 312–333.

Fayne, H., & Ortquist-Ahrens, L. (2006). Learning communities for first-year faculty: Transition, acculturation, and transformation. *To Improve the Academy, 24*(1), 277–290.

Jayakumar, U. M., Howard, T. C., Allen, W. R., & Han, J. C. (2009). Racial privilege in the professoriate: An exploration of campus climate, retention, and satisfaction. *Journal of Higher Education, 80*(5), 538–563.

Stanley, C. A. (2006). Coloring the academic landscape: Faculty of color breaking the silence in predominantly white colleges and universities. *Education & Educational Research, 43*(4), 701–736.

Tomlin, A. D. (Ed.). (2023). *Black faculty do it all: A moment in the life of a blackademic.* Information Age Publishing.

Tuitt, F., Hanna, M., Martinez, L. M., Salazar, M., & Griffin, R. (2009). Faculty of color in the academy: Teaching in the line of fire. *Thought and Action, 25,* 65–74.

# SECTION 1

IT'S NOT JUST WHAT YOU KNOW, BUT WHO YOU KNOW AND ARE CONNECTED TO

CHAPTER 1

# THE ARCHITECT AND THE MOTHERSCHOLAR: LESSONS IN THE ELUSIVE ART OF NETWORKING IN THE ACADEMY

Tierney B. Hinman
*Auburn University, USA*

## ABSTRACT

Networking plays a significant role in supporting faculty success by offering opportunities for building social capital, potentially impacting productivity in positive ways as defined by publications, presentations, grants, leadership positions, and other scholarly endeavors. However, research indicates that not all faculty members, particularly those who are underrepresented in the academy, are provided with equitable opportunities for networking, especially in informal spaces outside of the typical workday. This chapter explores my experience with networking, as one (white) motherscholar, and how I came to (re)construct my perception of what networking is and how it can be accomplished in academic spaces by drawing on the knowledge and skills I already possessed as a motherscholar. Specifically, I argue that the individual, unique identities of faculty that the academy de-legitimizes can and should be leveraged to navigate, in part, an institution that prioritizes productivity over humanizing practice. By sharing my story, I hope to contribute to the

*Faculty Success in the Academy*, pages 7–19
Copyright © 2026 by Emerald Publishing Limited
All rights of reproduction in any form reserved.
doi:10.1108/978-1-80592-287-220251002

momentum of a movement that resists the single story of who scholars in the academy are and should be. In this vein, I examine my own participation in an affinity group, including how it was formed and maintained, in relation to networking as (re)conceptualized to include both traditional definitions of productivity, as well as the overall wellbeing of individual members in the network. I conclude with some thoughts for faculty considering building an affinity group as part of their networking plan.

*Keywords:* Academia; higher education; motherscholar; networking; carework

## IN RECOGNITION OF UNANTICIPATED ACCOMPLISHMENTS

About a decade ago, early in my marriage and doctoral work and with only one kid in tow, my husband and I considered building our own home. Ever the engineer, he found some software for computer-aided design and tasked us with developing some potential blueprints we could use as a guide while we shopped for builders. It should have been easy. I possessed all the necessary architectural tools, including the ability to build and move walls; apply custom colors and materials to flooring, siding, and walls; choose and place appliances; and create a budget to keep us within cost limits. The program was supposedly intuitive, claiming to be easy to use for amateurs. I lasted about a week with it, after which I gave up trying to make the vision in my head match what appeared on the screen. I had all the parts I needed to be successful and the raceclass (Leonardo, 2012) privilege to consider building a possibility in the first place, but I could never make the parts into a cohesive whole and I shoved the plan for building a home somewhere into the back recesses of my mind, telling myself that I would have to get to it someday but that today was not that day.

Fast-forward a couple of years and those same feelings of frustration, inadequacy, and overwhelmingness emerged as I neared the end of my doctoral program and moved onto the job market. Once again, I had all the parts. I knew how important networking was to my success—to get a job, to boost productivity and get funding to get me to tenure, and to access national leadership roles that could build my reputation (e.g., Ansman et al., 2014; Austin & McDaniels, 2006; Blickle et al., 2009; Ibarra et al., 2005; Sargent & Waters, 2004). I tried networking. I read the books. I did the research. I organized a group of doctoral students and asked a well-known scholar in the field to speak to us about tips for networking. But it all felt either nebulous, like the titular *Inside Higher Ed* article "Networking: Just Do It" (Aguilar, 2018), or not particularly doable, at least for me. I could envision what networking should look like, but, in practice, it simply didn't work.

Following traditional advice, I did seek out leading scholars and search committee chairs at national conferences. The first time, I made it through an entire roundtable presentation without ever introducing myself or speaking to the person I had sought out. The next two times I managed to speak to the person, but only in passing and it was all very awkward, dissatisfying, and unproductive. It felt disingenuous to ask a question or express interest with the purpose of getting someone to know my name and I had no idea how to continue building that connection at other times and in other spaces. The whole process didn't feel like the true relationship-building I wanted to do.

There were additional layers, though. A leading scholar who agreed to meet with me to discuss my dissertation work but (understandably) only later in the evening. New faculty breakfasts and collaborative work times that were planned during school drop-off and pick-up times. Receptions, drinks, teambuilding, and knowledge building activities that occurred after-hours. As a mother of three also navigating mental health issues with a loved one, sometimes there was/is only me and work caves to caretaking.

I am not alone. Research on professional interactions (e.g., Hyers et al., 2012; Turner et al., 2008) suggests that meaningful networking is more likely to happen in these kinds of informal settings and yet women and other underrepresented faculty in academia are less likely to be present in these contexts, impacting the social capital they generate. I have spent a lot of time worrying about social capital and its effects on my potential tenure at an R1 university, as well as on my overall career trajectory. I waffle between feeling like Superwoman (Shaevitz, 1984) and feeling completely powerless, questioning my career choices, because in the end, my emotional, mental, and physical capacities are not limitless.

I don't expect the anxiousness or guilt I feel—for not being a better mother, for not being a better researcher or teacher—to ever go away completely. And yet, this past year I found myself leading a paper presentation at a national conference with a group of established scholars from universities across the United States while I rocked my 9-month-old to sleep. Our group had accrued a number of publications and a long list of conference presentations in the 5 years we had already worked together. They had encouraged my intellectual work, helping me establish key components of my scholarly identity, and mentored me into my first tenure-track appointment in the middle of a global pandemic. They had also sent me a text set of children's picture books when I had my third child and helped me navigate so many of the challenges of being a mother, especially when what I knew from my work in literacy education clashed with what I experienced with my children. It was messy, it was hard, and it was in that moment that my identity as a motherscholar (Matias, 2022) began to solidify.

I had unexpectedly accomplished what I had set out to do, establishing an emerging network—a constellation of mentors (Johnson, 2016) rather than a single mentor, each with their own kind of knowledge, experiences, and expertise—committed to supporting not only my professional growth but my personal health and wellbeing as well. It hadn't looked like I had thought it was supposed to. It wasn't nerve-racking one-on-one meetings or uncomfortable introductions at events where I felt out-of-place. It was Zoom meetings with three kids on the screen, a fly-by at a work session between teaching and school pick-up, and finishing a collaborative proposal at 2 a.m. because my daughter sat next to me with a stomach bug. I had cultivated a group of outstanding scholar-friends who challenged me to think more deeply and more critically about my work, strengthening my research and writing skills, while simultaneously adopting the role of "aunt" and picking up the toy my baby threw for the umpteenth time. The relationship was reciprocal. I had knowledge and experience to offer in my areas of expertise while I made space for all the identities that they brought into our relationship, some that we had in common (i.e., navigating a relationship with someone with mental health challenges) and some that we did not (i.e., raising twins). Like my foray into amateur architecture when my family considered building our home, the networking "program" I had been given didn't help me accomplish my vision despite all the tools it provided me because my personal and professional lives don't function separately. Instead, I leveraged the tools I had, stemming from my motherscholar identity, to rebuild my vision and construct a network, in reality this time, that nourished and sustained *all* aspects of my identities.

## NARRATIVE THEORY AS A TOOL FOR IDENTITY (RE) CONSTRUCTION

Rebuilding my relationship with networking became possible because I was able to (re)construct how I perceived and experienced the world through my emerging identity as a motherscholar. The kind of agency required for this act of (re)construction is born from my capacity to tell and retell stories about myself. Connelly and Clandinin (1990) argue that "people lead storied lives and tell stories about those lives" (p. 2) and it is through these stories that meaning gets attributed to our lives. Although the individual stories we tell can often seem fractured, incomplete, and even contradictory, these characteristics defining the telling of our stories indicate the ways in which the narratives we tell are dynamic, enduring, and multiply constructed (Bansel, 2013). Thus, narrative becomes a powerful tool through which we can (re)construct our identities (Ricoeur, 1988).

The term motherscholar itself is an example of how narrative (re)constructs identity. As separate terms, mother and scholar tell different stories about identity, ones that have been traditionally contradictory, existing in different spheres of daily life and possessing different relationships to power. When the terms are combined, however, a different story about identity is told as "both terms mother and scholar inform each other simultaneously, with equal weight, and from the same originating axis...conjoin[ing] together as one to make anew" (Matias, 2022, p. 247). Thus, mother and scholar occupy the same space, even when in tension, shaping and informing the lenses through which the world is perceived and experienced.

Narrative theory informs both the content and process of my scholarly work. When I conduct research with teachers and students, narrative theory guides me in recognizing their stories as their truth and valuing even the little stories they tell me as insights into the identities they are claiming, disclaiming, sitting in tension with, and rewriting. It helps me center their voice and acknowledge the agency they possess to tell their stories in their way while still recognizing that I hear and interpret their stories through the lenses of my own identities—as a motherscholar; as a white, female teacher educator; as a cisgender woman—and, thus, a new layer of their narrative (and mine) is constructed.

Through narrative, I understand that people are always becoming and I acknowledge that the same is true for me. As a perpetual work-in-progress, I can give myself (and others) grace to make and own up to mistakes, to be less than, and to not know. In a professional field that prizes a kind of singular-minded version of success defined by productivity, expertise, and *h*-indexes, narrative theory helps me humanize my own presence and that of others in academia, along with the work we do. It reminds me that it's not just the missed deadline but also the repair work I did on my relationship with my daughter after our fight. It's not just the journal rejection but also the time I'm spending watching a movie with my family rather than doing revisions. It's not just that I have met the quota for publications for tenure but that I'm doing research that centers stories and the ways that stories can expand our ways of seeing the world and act upon us to become agents of change in classrooms. I am all of my successes and failures according to the institution, but I am also more. This framing is particularly important when I find myself, as I sometimes do, feeling inadequate. It is why I, as a motherscholar, approach networking in alternative ways, seeking scholars who can be mentors, collaborators, and friends—people who can attend to my whole story and not just the parts of my story that are consistent with the dominant narratives that have been constructed around who scholars are and should be.

## (RE)NARRATING WORK IN ACADEMIA: WHAT I WISH I HAD KNOWN

In her 2022 introduction to a special issue on motherscholars and motherscholarship, Matias explained how she came to the identity of motherscholar while she was on the job market and her male mentor advised her not to reveal that she was a mother of twins. For many of us, this is a familiar refrain. I heard it, although, gratefully, not from my committee, when I went on the job market in 2019. I have attended numerous doctoral student advising sessions during which the same questions and advice arose. There were motherscholars, though, who always resisted this narrative. In consonance with these scholars, Matias (2022) wrote:

> I refused to negate that which makes me whole. Instead of being hard-headed, I simply was tired of feeling ashamed of acknowledging and loving someone(s) that has/have made me me; something that has made me the loving, forgiving, and understanding person I need to be in order to do the exemplary academic work my institution so demands. I am sure this fact resonates with all motherscholars. Being a mother was never a hindrance…only the academy's refusal to acknowledge its complexity and truly honor and accommodate its diversity was. (p. 250)

In refusing to acknowledge the mother part of my motherscholar identity, the academy worked to limit the tools I had at my disposal to support my success in academia, sending the message that, as a mother, academia was not a place in which I belonged. I wish I had known, or perhaps that I had had the fortitude, to recognize and leverage much earlier my full identity as a motherscholar to validate the tools that I already possessed and that became available to me *because of* my motherscholar identity. That is not to say that I think that having more confidence or strength or hard-headedness will erase the systemic oppression at play in the academy, particularly because I recognize that other parts of my identity come with privileges. Rather, it is about wishing that I had known that I could let my identity as a motherscholar shape more about how I navigated the spaces of the academy. I have a lot to learn, *and* I possess knowledge and skills already that can inform how and why I research, teach, and build collaborations and relationships. Advice, like that on networking, is just that—advice. It is not an exhaustive or lockstep list dictating what I *must* do if I plan on surviving, and even flourishing, in academia. There exists, because of the identities I possess, more than one way. I did not have to erase part of my identity when in certain academic spaces; I could, in fact, be both the architect and the motherscholar, leveraging my identity to (re)narrate what it means to be in and do the work of academia.

## (RE)DESIGNING NETWORKING FOR SUCCESS

Part of narrating a new story about how I could participate in the academy as a motherscholar included (re)designing how I thought about networking in ways that could support my success. For me, success is more than just productivity (Institutional expectations around productivity for tenure ensure that it remains central). Instead, I also consider success to be finding overall meaning, purpose, and joy in the work that I do. It is about growing my emotional, intellectual, mental, and spiritual health and, although I can do a bit of that individually, it is heavily dependent upon the building of relationships—the right kind of relationships—that can sustain me through the hard work.

I think the idea behind networking has always been about relationship-building, but I needed more than just getting my name and my work known. I could, and on occasion did, meet one-on-one with well-known scholars to ask a question about my work or their work, but, particularly because I found it hard to be in those informal spaces often, they were always one-off meetings and it seemed disingenuous to try to do more. Instead, I needed to build relationships that made space for my motherscholar identity, relationships I could form in less traditional spaces and in which I could seek feedback, advice, and emotional support without concern of professional penalty or image maintenance.

This kind of relationship-building emerged from a more organic approach to networking. It was following up, by email, on ideas privately messaged to me on a methodological framework during a paper presentation at a national conference that was held on Zoom during the height of the pandemic. It was finding similarities across presentations a scholar and I had given at the same conference session and floating the idea of a joint project. One of the most impactful decisions I made for networking was to attend a study group (i.e., the Teacher Education Research Study Group) held during the annual conference for the Literacy Research Association, a large national organization in my field. The study group, held over lunch, was a more informal meeting of scholars interested in collaborative work and was intentionally designed to help scholars find affinity groups based on research interests and facilitate the conceptualization of an emerging project that could lead to conference presentations, grants, and publications. Over the course of three days, the group facilitators helped generate a list of research interests, form small groups around those interests, and begin planning a research study using a template provided to guide discussion about study design and individual responsibilities. It was during that meeting that, as a doctoral student, I met six female scholars who would end up forming the foundation of my mentoring constellation.

It wasn't quite as straightforward and simple as it sounds. In the first year of my collaborative work with the group, I nearly dropped out because I felt so inadequate next to the six tenured and tenure-track faculty members who comprised the group. I was just a doctoral student getting use to the hierarchy of higher education programs and they had publications, experience, grants, and leadership roles; I questioned what knowledge or skills I possessed that could possibly benefit them. Participation in the group also took time and effort; we met on Zoom for several hours once a month to read, write, and think together. Committing to attending was challenging and I often participated by car as I drove the 75-minute commute to the university or as I fed my kids their lunch.

Eventually, though, as we spent time together, the six women in this cross-institutional group became irreplaceable, in both my personal and professional spheres. They helped me prepare for my first interviews and encouraged me as I navigated the job market, wrote my dissertation, and raised young children. They were my touchstones during my first year on the tenure-track during the height of the pandemic when I had so little contact with people in my own department. They modeled phenomenal scholarly work for me and mentored me into leading my own projects with the group. They answered my questions (truthfully and kindly), they connected me with resources, and they checked in with me. It was less about shared identities (e.g., not all of them are motherscholars, although we do have some shared identity markers), and more about the kind of people they are and the nurturing approach they take to mentoring by taking into consideration the whole of my story. By considering my whole story, they made space for me to begin building a scholarly identity through my work that goes beyond metrics and focuses on its overarching purpose in ways that guide how I make decisions about what research, collaborative work, outreach, and other projects I participate in.

The group has been productive in terms of presentations and publications, including ones in high-impact journals, and they are currently helping me navigate into national leadership roles. At the same time, we've nurtured joy and wellbeing, supporting one another through the pandemic shutdown, holding space in moments of individual crisis, and welcoming celebrations of all of life's big and small accomplishments. We meet when we can at conferences, in both formal presentation spaces and for drinks afterward. Our group holds monthly meetings on Zoom (and from three of the four US mainland time zones). We do the logistical work of figuring out how our group will function together and the intellectual work of designing and carrying out projects, but we also do relational work. The first part of our meetings are always check-ins and one of our favorite all-time meetups was our Zoom Happy Hour held during the pandemic shutdown. We are cross-institutional, creating a space for each of us to grow and challenge each other without concerns for image maintenance. Leadership roles are flexible and rotating, not dependent upon rank, and provide opportunities for everyone to step-up, as well as temporarily step-out when professional and/or personal demands are too pressing.

While the success of the group is, at least relationally, partly due to the nature of our work (i.e., self-study of teacher education practices in antiracism), the rest is replicable in some fashion across fields in academia. Therefore, I suggest faculty members identify new networking opportunities. Check with professional organizations for these kind of informal working/study groups inside formal spaces (e.g., a conference). Since the start of the pandemic, opportunities to participate virtually have increased dramatically, making them more accessible for those who find travel difficult. However, affinity groups can be formed just by seeking out those with shared interests in any formal or informal space. The last section of this chapter provides several tips to consider when networking to form an affinity group. However, remember that your identities may grant you unique tools, so don't be afraid to be your own architect in (re)designing a network path.

## TIPS FOR (RE)DESIGNING AFFINITY GROUPS

1. *Be particular about who you form collaborations with when creating an affinity group.* Sometimes, the pressures of academia make us forget that networking is about more than prestige. Seek people who hold space for all of your story, whatever it may be, and fully commit to those people who consider one another's emotional, intellectual, mental, and spiritual wellbeing.
2. *At some point, you'll need to make the decision to quit or continue with a group.* All collaborations go through an awkward stage as purpose and roles are negotiated. For example, writing productivity might be initially slower while project leadership is unclear, but the right group eventually finds some measure of stability through explicit discussion of group leadership and authorship order in relation to responsibilities in the research and writing process.
3. *It's likely everyone in the group is feeling inadequate in one way or another.* These inadequacies often include not feeling smart enough, not writing well enough, or not knowing enough and are often tied to institutional expectations for expertise (i.e., product) and not the real demands of engaging in the process of designing, conducting, and writing up research. Don't let your feelings of inadequacy stop you from accepting leadership and mentorship and offering the same. The right group will help you recognize your own strengths

(e.g., writing, organizing, communicating) while you leverage theirs through your collaborative work.
4. *Time is finite, but don't forgo the relational work in place of the purely logistical/intellectual.* The relational work is what sustains long-term intellectual work because you are now also accountable to people who matter to you. It allows for deeper intellectual work that survives the conflicts that inevitably arise in collaborative work. Rather than ignoring the obstacles, whether individual (i.e., family issues) or collective (i.e., differences in ideology), the relational works to problem solve so attention can return to the intellectual. Additionally, it's in the relational work that you can learn from others—about what it's like to go through the tenure process, about what you should consider when choosing a journal, or about where you might begin the process of navigating into a national leadership role.
5. *There is a reason for a networking constellation.* Not everyone can be everything all the time and you'll find that different people will be better sources of information on different aspects of being in the academy. For example, one person might understand what it means to be a mother in the academy while someone else has more experience navigating into national leadership roles and someone else is a better sounding board for new project ideas. Cultivate a diverse group of mentors/collaborators and draw on their individual strengths.

## REFERENCES

Aguilar, S. J. (2018, June 27). Networking: Just do it. *Inside Higher Ed.* https://www.insidehighered.com/advice/2018/06/28/getting-past-common-obstacles-effective-networking-early-tenure-track-opinion

Ansman, L., Flichinger, T. E., Barello, S., Kunneman, M., Mantwill, S., Quilligan, S., Zanini, C., & Aelbrecht, K. (2014). Career development for early career academics: Benefits of networking and the role of professional societies. *Patient Education and Counseling, 97*(1), 132–134.

Austin, A. E., & McDaniels, M. (2006). Preparing the professoriate of the future: Grade student socialization for faculty roles. In J. C. Smart (Ed.), *Higher education: Handbook of theory and research* (pp. 397–456). Springer.

Bansel, P. (2013). Same but different: Space, time and narrative. *Literacy, 47,* 4–9.

Blickle, G., Witzki, A. H., & Schneider, P. B. (2009). Mentoring support and power: A three year predictive field study on protégé networking and career success. *Journal of Vocational Behavior, 74,* 181–189.

Connelly, M., & Clandinin, J. (1990). Stories of experience and narrative inquiry. *Educational Researcher, 19*(5), 2–14.

Hyers, L. L., Sypha, J., Cochran, K., & Brown, T. (2012). Disparities in the professional development interactions of university faculty as a function of gender and ethnic underrepresentation. *The Journal of Faculty Development, 26*(1), 18–28.

Ibarra, H., Kilduff, M., & Tsai, W. (2005). Zooming in and out: Connecting individual and collectivities at the frontiers of organizational network research. *Organization Science, 16*, 359–371.

Johnson, W. B. (2016). *On being a mentor: A guide for higher education faculty.* Routledge.

Leonardo, Z. (2012). The race for class: Reflections on a critical race theory of education. *Educational Studies, 48*(5), 427–449.

Matias, C. E. (2022). Birthing the motherscholar and motherscholarship. *Peabody Journal of Education, 97*(2), 246–250.

Ricoeur, P. (1988). *Time and narrative.* University of Chicago Press.

Sargent, L. D., & Waters, L. D. (2004). Careers and academic research collaborations: An inductive framework for understanding successful collaborations. *Journal of Vocational Behavior, 64*, 308–319.

Shaevitz, M. H. (1984). *The superwoman syndrome.* Warner Publications.

Turner, C. S., González, J. C., & Wood, J. L. (2008). Faculty of color in academe: What 20 years of literature tells us. *Journal of Diversity in Higher Education, 1*, 139–168.

CHAPTER 2

# BUILDING INTENTIONAL COMMUNITY AND SUPPORT

**Kimberly M. Baker**
*University of Northern Iowa, USA*

### ABSTRACT

Faculty development often focuses on the individual level, noting the steps that faculty members can take to advance themselves. One component of professional development that is often missing is the role that community plays in advancing our careers. We benefit from testing new ideas with others, support and guidance from those we trust, and solidarity with people who share our circumstances. While community is important, not all groups are helpful as we progress through our careers. A group might not fit our needs, a group may contain members that are not supportive, or we might outgrow a group that once worked well for us. So, as we look for communities to help advance our professional growth, it is important to be intentional in finding groups that align with our needs and futures. This chapter emphasizes the importance of intentionally developing communities as a component of professional development. Such groups include Professional Learning Networks (PLNs), affinity groups, and book groups. These groups are a useful way to connect with others around various professional issues and can help us develop a sense of community with others in our profession. The main purpose of this chapter is to help faculty intentionally build community groups as a component of professional development.

*Keywords:* Community; professional development; faculty development; higher education; historically excluded faculty

## DISCOVERING I NEEDED COMMUNITY

When I started my first tenure-track position, I assumed I would stay for the duration of my career. My first job, however, had some unexpected challenges. The school had financial difficulties and an uncertain future. The department I was in had quite a bit of turmoil. I also struggled as a scholar who was trained at a research-intensive resource-rich university but now working in a very different environment. While I was struggling a lot in those early years, I felt like I had to navigate these challenges mostly on my own. Some of this feeling came from how my work was structured at the university. I was at a teaching-intensive college, and I viewed teaching as an individual enterprise. I was a qualitative researcher, and I expected to be writing mostly on my own. Reinforcing this sense of individual responsibility, I was evaluated for tenure and promotion as an individual. In addition to the conditions of my job, as a new professor from a working-class background, I was struggling with imposter syndrome—the feeling that I was not really qualified to be a professor. So, I feared reaching out to ask for help when I needed it.

Looking back, I can see now that in trying to do everything on my own, I was actually putting up barriers to building a sense of connection and belonging with those around me. I did have mentors, and they were great for giving guidance and helping me make connections, but they were not a source of solidarity for me. I did have friends that I talked with about things I was doing, but I did not often open up about how intensely I was struggling to settle in. I worked hard to manage the impression I knew what I was doing. Honestly, after a few years of trying to do everything on my own, I was exhausted. I was also not very happy.

Something needed to change, and since going it alone was not working, I decided to try a different approach. I considered what groups I was already involved in that I could envision as communities for me. I served on a committee of people I respected, I had attended multiple sessions with the teaching center, and I had some ties to a group of faculty in an academic area I valued. These groups were my starting points and all had some sense of community. While previously I attended meetings and socialized with people in these groups, I was not invested in them as communities. I also think these communities saw me as an attendee, but not necessarily a community member. So, I had to put in the effort to show up, to engage with others, and sometimes to be vulnerable. It was not an easy process and not all of these communities provided the support I needed, but along the way I realized that my professional development required communities. I found a few different people I felt I could trust on my campus and through my professional associations. Those people opened up to me and I in turn started to share more about myself. I found that the struggles I was having were not only mine, but actually pretty common.

I realized that one thing I could try to change was the place where I worked. The conditions of my department, the struggles of the school, and the balance of my workload were not situations that were going to change in my job, so I set out to see if I could change jobs. I found that the communities I was a part of were incredibly important to me as I started to look for other jobs. These communities helped guide me on how to go on the market quietly, to protect myself as a pre-tenure faculty member. Senior faculty from these communities agreed to serve as recommenders. And these communities became places I could turn to as I navigated a job market still rebounding from the 2008 economic crisis. These communities were central in helping me to achieve one of my most important accomplishments, being able to find a new academic appointment at a different institution.

## LOCATING MY SCHOLARLY WORK IN COMMUNITY

As a sociologist who focuses on deviance and social control, I study how groups achieve and enforce conformity and respond to those who do not fit in. That deviance and social control became the focus of my work is no accident. I grew up in a small town in a tightly knit religious community, and much of my early life I struggled to fit in. Early on I began imagining what my life could be like outside of this region and religious group. Of course, striking out is difficult as I was unfamiliar with communities outside of what I knew growing up. The separation was difficult, and I often felt very much on my own. So, as an academic-in-training, I was attracted to scholars like Goffman (1959) and Foucault (2012) who studied how conformity is enacted and enforced in everyday life.

These experiences and research interests can make me skeptical of groups and hesitant to join new ones. At the same time, I also know as humans we are social beings who need connections and that isolation can have devastating consequences (Putnam, 2020). Beyond attachments and groups, communities give us a sense of solidarity and purpose. Bruhn (2011) argues that community "implies a degree of consistency in fellowship and belongingness among members" and that this sense emerges from the feeling that we choose to be a part of the communities we join (p. 13). Palmer (2009) has called attention to the role that community plays in developing our craft as teachers. When community is purposefully built into faculty development, it can also improve our feeling of connectedness to our workplaces (Eib & Miller, 2006) and work toward change within those institutions (Bond & Blevins, 2020).

## WHAT I WISH I KNEW EARLY ON

Early in my career, I wish I had understood the importance of community for my professional advancement. I thought of groups primarily in support terms, like-minded people with whom I could share my experiences and get encouragement and advice. I had friends from graduate school, and I made friends at my new job and these were the primary people I thought about in times of need. I also understood the importance of mentors for helping me make connections, solve problems, and plan for the future. Frankly, I turned to my friends and mentors in similar ways. I would vent to them when I encountered frustrating experiences, and I would ask for their guidance when I did not know how to proceed.

Communities focused on professional development, however, are distinct from both friendship support groups and mentors in important ways. First, they are intentional. Professional development communities should have a stated purpose or goals (Parker, 2018). These communities could intend to help participants build networks across the profession, improve the quality of scholarship, prepare grant applications, and so on. Even less formal book groups, writing groups, and co-working groups should still have a clearly stated purpose. The key feature, regardless, is that they have identifiable goals at the outset. This purpose helps potential members know if the group could be a good fit and also keep the work of the group on track.

Second, professional development communities should articulate who fits within the group. Some groups are only for early-career faculty while others may include faculty from a range of career statuses. A group may be for a particular school, a professional organization, or some common interest. Groups may be only for faculty while others may include staff, community members, students, etc. Some groups may focus on particular interest or policy, such as faculty seeking to change the university's family leave policy. While other groups could be designated to include members with particular characteristics, such as affinity groups for Black faculty and LGBTQIIA+ faculty. In any case, the group should be able to articulate appropriate membership so that everyone has clear expectations for who fits in the group and, frankly, who does not.

Third, the community should have a designated schedule so that members know when the group will be meeting. Some groups may meet only for a few sessions for a short period. Other groups may be more open-ended, expecting members to rotate in and out over an extended period of time. Some groups may have a set schedule (e.g. every first Tuesday of the month at noon). Other groups may select times based on member availability. A good professional development group will articulate the schedule plan clearly so that members can decide if the group fits their availability. A group might fit in terms of purpose and membership, but if the faculty member cannot attend any sessions, then joining will have no benefit.

## RECOMMENDED OPPORTUNITIES FOR NEW FACULTY MEMBERS

One place to start in the search for new communities is to look for professional development workshops and groups seeking new members. These opportunities may be a single meeting or may meet over an extended period of time. Some of these opportunities may require some effort to locate. For example, it is worth searching in different parts of campus, such as the teaching center, the office of research, the graduate college, and other academic colleges/schools across campus. These options may occur in parts of campus for which you are not automatically added to the email listserv when you arrive, so you may not learn about these options organically. These kinds of opportunities are important for the content of the workshop, but also an opportunity to meet others on campus and to learn more about what is happening at your campus. I have found that sometimes these opportunities are also associated with additional pay or other perks. For example, my campus has offered summer workshop series on course design, grant writing, and service learning that receive stipends for completed work.

I also recommend looking for professional development opportunities beyond your campus. It is likely your national professional association offers early career professional development opportunities (sometimes during the year and sometimes at the annual meeting). Also, look for opportunities at regional associations in your area. Regional associations are often smaller, easier for early career faculty to gain access, and less expensive to attend. Their annual meetings will often include professional development sessions. For example, I've attended several sessions on our regional journal with the editors that have been incredibly helpful. There are also some paid professional development options that can be worth it. For several years, I was an off-and-on member of Academic Ladder, an organization that offers one-on-one coaching and small group accountability to help faculty increase their writing productivity. Another organization is the National Center for Faculty Development & Diversity (NCFDD) which offers a variety of mentoring programs focused on writing and productivity. Some faculty may be able to access NCFDD opportunities through their university's membership, while others may need to join individually for access. There are also a variety of coaching and consulting businesses offering to support faculty development. It is worth checking with your department head or dean to find out if your school will help pay for these options.

These kinds of professional development opportunities can be helpful in lots of ways. Most obviously, the content of the sessions can be practically helpful as we develop our independence as a scholar and faculty member. Toward this end, it is worth looking for opportunities that fit your needs and interests. In addition, attending these sessions on campus and in your region can help you better understand the specific context of your work. Many of us move far from the location of our graduate training and also work at different types of institutions. Learning the specifics of our work expectations and conditions and how they're different from our graduate institutions is valuable. Third, these professional development opportunities offer a time to build connections. You may meet other faculty members with similar interests, you may meet people who can help you make connections to valuable resources, you can find mentors, and you can begin building a sense of community. Most professional development opportunities will not immediately give you a sense of community—which can take a while to build. Starting early, however, will help new faculty plant seeds for communities that can flourish later.

## FIVE TIPS FOR FACULTY SUCCESS

Here are my top five recommendations for faculty success with a commitment to being in community:

1. *Find professional development groups early*—When you start your first academic appointment, look for professional development opportunities. Be intentional about the groups and workshops you seek out. Look for ones that fit your interests and seem relevant to your career goals.
2. *Look for groups that do not include your evaluators*—During your early career, you will be evaluated persistently by people on your tenure review committee, your department head, senior colleagues in your area, etc. It is important to be aware of this kind of scrutiny because it may mean that these individuals are not safe to confide in regarding your struggles and challenges. Look for groups that do not include your evaluators and with whom you can more comfortably confide in when you need it.
3. *Stay focused on your professional goals*—It is so easy to get sidetracked. I think it is especially easy if you are from historically excluded groups. Committees and leaders will seek you out to serve extensively, students from similar backgrounds can easily feel attached to you, and lots of opportunities will surface that distract from your professional plans. I recommend writing down your professional goals and periodically revisiting them, to remind you of your path. It is okay to change your goals (probably even good to do so), but do so because you are being purposeful rather than being pulled along other paths.

4. *Protect your time*—Along with focusing on your goals, be fiercely protective of how you allocate your time. To do so, you will have to get very good at saying no. It can be hard at first, especially if you have any people-pleasing leanings. I recommend finding people you trust that you can reach out to when you are offered new opportunities. Tell them your goals and discuss whether these opportunities keep you on track. Practice turning down opportunities and standing firms when the person offering you an "opportunity" does not accept your first no. With practice, it gets easier to protect your time (and also those around you learn to take you at your word).
5. *Keep a journal or journal to document your professional development activities*—These activities can often be invisible. Maintaining some kind of documentation of your professional development participation can help you make this work visible. In tracking these efforts, you can also more intentionally reflect on the professional development work you are doing and make periodic adjustments. Additionally, making this work visible can help you document the professional development work you are doing for tenure and promotion files.

## CONCLUSION

Professional development is a process we cannot achieve on our own. We need others to support and collaborate with us as we grow professionally. Finding groups that align with our professional views is a good starting point, but a sense of community will not develop for us in all groups. We benefit from testing new ideas with others, support and guidance from those we trust, and solidarity with people who share our circumstances. This chapter has emphasized the importance of intentionally and actively building communities to fit our professional needs and goals. At times, we may need to create groups when we cannot find what we need, and we may need to leave groups that no longer serve us. The larger goal, however, should be to find communities we can engage with, contribute to, and benefit from as we progress in our careers.

## REFERENCES

Bond, M. A., & Blevins, S. J. (2020). Using faculty professional development to foster organizational change: A social learning framework. *TechTrends, 64*(2), 229–237. https://doi.org/10.1007/s11528-019-00459-2

Bruhn, J. G. (2011). *The sociology of community connections.* Springer Science & Business Media.

Eib, B. J., & Miller, P. (2006). Faculty development as community building—An approach to professional development that supports communities of practice for online teaching. *The International Review of Research in Open and Distributed Learning, 7*(2). https://doi.org/10.19173/irrodl.v7i2.299

Foucault, M. (2012). *Discipline and punish: The birth of the prison.* Knopf Doubleday Publishing Group.

Goffman, E. (1959). *The presentation of self in everyday life.* Knopf Doubleday Publishing Group.

Palmer, P. J. (2009). *The courage to teach: Exploring the inner landscape of a teacher's life.* John Wiley & Sons.

Parker, P. (2018). *The art of gathering: How we meet and why it matters.* Penguin.

Putnam, R. D. (2020). *Bowling alone: Revised and updated: The collapse and revival of American community.* Simon & Schuster.

CHAPTER 3

# FACULTY SUCCESS: A PATH WORTH TRAVELING

**Mary E. Robinson**
*Montgomery College, USA*

### ABSTRACT

This chapter discusses a reflection of fears about whether or not to pursue a career in higher education. The subsections glean insights into the theory that aligns my scholarly activities and the role networking, mentoring and professional development play within higher education success. Each of these three can highly contribute to shaping one's career path. As such, this chapter provides insight into the value of and the benefits that networking and professional development had on my career path and future aspirations. The chapter ends with five salient points for faculty success.

*Keywords:* Career path; faculty; leadership; networking; mentorship; self-actualize

### FROM FEAR TO FACULTY OF THE YEAR

For some people, the pursuit of higher education is one aspect of the American Dream. In high school despite athletic scholarships for Track and Volleyball I did not foresee the possibility of attending college. Mainly, I was not knowledgeable about college funding. I was fearful of several what if's, i.e., what if I do not have enough scholarship funds to pay for my entire tuition including books? What if I do not have enough scholarship funds to cover the expenses for college housing? In high school, I did not receive financial aid literacy information nor did my parents. I recall my parents not understanding why they would need to provide tax information to complete the Free Application for Federal Student Aid (FAFSA) form? The irony of the question was not so much about privacy of personal information as it was the connection between tax forms and a student's FAFSA form. The lack of knowledge about attending college is a barrier for many. Brown et al. (2021) aptly shared the following:

> First Generation (FG) students are less likely to have family members who know that waivers exist to pay for the ACT or SAT and are less likely to complete the Free Application for Federal Students Aid (FAFSA) because of uncertainty about their or other family members' status as an immigrant, or because their parents are fearful of being audited by the IRS or ashamed of their financial position. (p. 45)

As such, the desire for me to attend college diminished and I obtained a job with the Federal Government. Even though I obtained a job with the Federal Government I still had a desire to pursue higher education. As a result of sharing my higher education goals with others, I was fortunate through extended church family to consider attending Barber-Scotia College (BSC) in Concord, North Carolina. With the opportunity to attend college I dealt with reservations and fears such as leaving Maryland and navigating the college admission processes. By sharing my reservations, I had no idea that my extended family was in communication with a BSC college admission counselor, who guided my entire admission processes including selecting Business Administration with a focus in Accounting as my Bachelor of Science (BS) major. As time was leading up to leaving for college, I was informed that my tuition was paid for 3 years leaving only 1 year of financial aid funding needed to earn a degree. I am grateful for the extended family of mentors, who highly contributed to my ability to pursue higher education. As I dripped in tears about leaving my sister and Mom in Maryland, the designated driver drove me to college, and I was left at the gutter of Higher Education. Nonetheless, the impact of mentorship has been valuable throughout my life. I am very humble to say that I am most proud of completing my BS degree as opposed to getting on the Greyhound Bus to return back to Maryland. After completing my BS degree, I pursued a Master of Science (MS) Degree in Special Education at Coppin State University; Masters in Pastoral Counseling from Loyal College in Maryland, and a Doctorate in Higher Education, (EdD) from Morgan State University.

I am glad that I overcame my fears to attend college. I never thought that the pathway from undergraduate to graduate would lead to a role in teaching high school and later college. These experiences ultimately led to my greatest achievement so far, being named the 2021 Montgomery College in Maryland Faculty of the Year.

## PRESENCE MATTERS

One theory that aligns with my scholarly activities is Carl Rogers (1980) Way of Being. Rogers's theory focuses on self-concept, self-worth, and the ideal self. His approach was one of being client-centered to help people self-actualize or work toward reaching their full unique potential. Since I teach in multiple modalities (online, remote and face-to-face), I strive to ensure that way of being creates a sense of presence whether face-to-face or teaching online. In my day-to-day scholarly work, I hope that some portion of what I do, whether facilitating a course, leading a small group as in my 2022 *Interactive Presentation on Team Building: Implementing the 4 Group Dynamics Plus 1 in a Virtual Workplace*, serving as a faculty member on college-level committees, mentoring new faculty, may impact one's life.

## ASKING QUESTIONS MATTERS

A career path is not always a one-way proposition. However, I wish that I knew the importance of honing in on a career path and pursuing opportunities within that field, which would have led to retirement at an earlier age. There is no policy against pursuing other career paths, but I do wish that I understood the value of in-house professional development and on the job training opportunities. I agree with the idea of Andri and Mandataris (2023), who believed on the job training can have a positive impact on an individual's work performance. Since I did not attend college immediately after high school, emerging from high school to work for the Federal Government was a proud accomplishment. Yet, it was not admirable within my peer circle. The position with the Federal Government meant that I had to rise early at 4.00 a.m. to be on the shuttle van by 5.30 a.m. By the time I got home in the evenings I did not have much time to socialize with friends. Therefore, I left the Federal Government position and pursued a job closer to home. Even though I pursued a job closer to home, I wanted to acquire a solid career position. As the era of "to believer or not believe in role models" emerged I read several leadership books, attended job training workshops, kept a journal and soon after earning my BS, I charted my path to the arena of teaching.

If I had to begin again, I would have made connections with other employees on the commuter van to ask questions about their roles in the Federal Government. During my time at the Federal Government search engines and checking websites was not prevalent but my lack of motivation to make connections was stifled by not reaching out to ask questions. While exploring other career fields is relevant—I simply did not consider the professional development opportunities to prepare me for other next-level positions within the Federal Government. The opportunity to do online professional development was not an option and staying after work would have meant that I would miss the commuter van. Weighing obstacles to enhancing a career field should be taken into consideration in order to identify support systems or resources needed to engage in workplace opportunities. I pondered leaving the Federal Government because I could not visual myself beyond the entry level position.

Years later, I started working in the field of Education. I researched other career opportunities and the required trajectories. In addition, I attended professional development training, leadership institutes, and acquired graduate level-higher education to prepare me for next-level positions. However, it is important to note that the benefit of collaborating with a teacher mentor was extremely helpful in my educational career development. The teacher mentor held new teachers accountable for attending after school and or weekend workshops. In fact, the teacher mentor helped me to plot my future career paths in education. As a result, I reviewed next level job positions, and I became aware of the required knowledge, skills, and abilities needed. I asked to shadow other senior administrators to acquire insight into other fields. According to Basariya and Sree (2019) there are pros and cons about on-the-job training. I believe that inquiring about such opportunities would have enticed me to continue working with the Federal Government but equally on-the-job training in education have allowed me success in higher education.

## MENTORING MATTERS

The first opportunity I would suggest to faculty members is to explore external partnerships with entities in higher education. Most new faculty early in their career are not focused on connecting with external partnerships, however, these can be both enriching and rewarding. Connecting with external partnerships does have cost implications but, the benefits of belonging far outweigh the cost. In fact, my suggestion is to check with your institution about memberships that may be financially covered. Connections with Professional Organizations such as the American Research Education Association (AERA), National Student Success Organization (NOSS),

American Association of Community Colleges (AACC), National Council of Black American Affairs (NCBAA) highly contributed to my s scholarship of teaching and leadership as a faculty leader. AACC offers a yearly Future Leadership Institute (FLI) and NCBAA offers a Mid-Manager Leadership Development Institute. Each Institute provided leadership skills that helpful in my role as a Department Chair.

A second opportunity I would suggest is to always continue learning. The pursuit of internal and external professional development opportunities is vital, particularly teaching fellowships, attending conferences, and leadership institutes. Ascione et al. (2022) suggested that faculty development can offer faculty the opportunity to participate in structured individual interaction, team building exercises including social learning, and learning activities among a diverse set of participants. Attending external professional development training sessions is insightful but more importantly one can glean educational tips and strategies to continuously develop as a faculty member.

Another no cost career enhancement opportunity relates to joining a listserv. Joining listserv does not correlate with years of service as a faculty member. Anyone can join a listserv such as the Association for Academic Leaders, which provides updated trends and fads in one's discipline. The incoming emails can provide leads to additional membership beyond the institution's connections as well as insight into journal articles and or blogs which are all relevant enhancements that foster faculty development. There are endless indirect mentoring opportunities in addition to a listserv. Indirect mentoring requires the self-initiative to subscribe to networks lead by professional and nonprofessionals. The Gates Notes my Bill Gates is a weekly Blog with a broad range of topics, Minute with Maxwell offers weekly Leadership Lessons and Master Classes from leaders such as Felicia Guity.

## SHINE! FIVE TIPS FOR FACULTY SUCCESS

The arena of higher education is complex. Yet as a faculty member I suggest other faculty members enjoy the field and remember to **SHINE!**

> *Seek mentorship.* Mentorship is the most valuable asset to a faculty member. Mentorship internal to the institution is beneficial and rewarding especially for new faculty. The benefits are endless! For example, as a new faculty member I was paired with a seasoned faculty member, who reviewed my course syllabus, gave a tour of the campus, provided insight into campus resources for students and vital to my course, such as the Writing, Reading, and Language Center (WRLC). Mentorship externally helps to provide guidance

and support that one may not acquire from internal support and resources. I recall that one of my favorite leadership books, Leadership Secrets of Squirrels came from a recommendation of an external mentor who I met at a conference round-table discussion. The book was particularly helpful in my decision-making process to pursue the role of Department Chair.

*Help others.* The opportunity to gain experience as a faculty member may not always come from acquiring additional education, being a mentee, or receiving internal recognition. Dismissing the need to reach back and help others is rewarding. Whether you seek community work locally or nationally the benefits of helping others far outweigh the commitment of time. Remember larger organizations such as the American Red Cross, State Special Olympics, or Habitat for Humanity projects can count as service opportunities.

*Inquire about opportunities.* Beyond the faculty evaluation post dialog with a Department Chair or Dean, faculty should take the initiative to inquire about internal opportunities, such as joining or being nominated for internal institutional committees. By volunteering to serve on institutional committees a faculty member gains insight into the organizational aspects of the college. The experience gained by serving on committees such as an internal Academic Master Plan Committee, Collegewide Governance or Strategic Planning Committees can also contribute to one's leadership skills for future career aspirations.

*Network.* Networking is different from Mentorship. Networking is about building relationships within your field and beyond. Networking is not all about academic circles. The exchange of a physical or digital business card or social media tags enhances one's personal life and professional connections. By networking you may connect with someone who can share further insight into helping you accomplish an academic goal, offer assistance in reviewing your resume/CV, and even connect you with other professional organizations.

*Evaluate yourself.* Some of the most valuable lessons that have contributed to my toolbox are from the feedback of student course evaluations and feedback from classroom observations through the lens of the Discipline Dean, Chair and Faculty Colleagues. Valuing student feedback, opinions, and perspectives through the lens of someone else is a quality control check-up. Take advantage of such feedback to evaluate yourself at the end of every semester to craft your next semester's lessons and one's personal career obligations. By doing so, you are assured to not become stagnant in your field of work as observations provide educational tips and strategies to continuously grow as faculty members.

Finally, never stop learning. Anthony J. D'Angelo aptly stated, **"Develop a passion for learning. If you do, you will never cease to grow"** (Anthony J.D'Angelo Quotes, n.d.).

## REFERENCES

Andri, S., & Mandataris, M. (2023). The effect of job training, job supervision and employee commitment to job performance. *Jurnal Pamator: Jurnal Ilmiah Universitas Trunojoyo, 16*(2), 377–385.

Anthony J.D'Angelo Quotes. (n.d.). BrainyQuote.com. https://www.brainyquote.com/quotes/anthony_j_dangelo_153989

Ascione, F. J., Daniels, T., Najjar, G., Patterson, V., & Stalburg, C. M. (2022). Evaluating the effectiveness of an intensive faculty development program based on the community of practice model. *Journal of Interprofessional Education & Practice, 26*, 100486.

Basariya, R. S., & Sree, V. (2019). Pros and cons of on-the-job training versus off the job training. *International Journal of Scientific & Technology Research, 8*(10), 671–674.

Brown, C., Reeves, A., & Puchner, L. (2021). College access for prospective first-generation high school students: Parent perceptions. *Journal of College Access, 6*(1).

Rogers, C. R. (1980). *A way of being*. Houghton Mifflin.

## ADDITIONAL READING

Robinson, M. (2022). *An interactive presentation on team building: Implementing the 4 group dynamics plus 1 in a virtual workplace*. Maryland Education Opportunity Center.

CHAPTER 4

# THIS WHAT GOT ME THRU": BLACK MOTHERING, OTHERMOTHERING, AND FURTHERMOTHERING IN ACADEMIA

**Amir Asim Gilmore**
*Washington State University, USA*

### ABSTRACT

This is not a story about grit and determination but the significance of mothering, othermothering, and further mothering in academia. The concept of mothering extends beyond birthmothers and is a survival mechanism for children's physical and emotional well-being. Professors take up that responsibility in educational institutions as a critical intervention against Black students' subjection. While mothering does not dismantle power systems in academia, its notions of sharing, caring, love, communion, and guardianship provide a small wake for Black students to achieve academic success. Toward this end, this chapter critically examines the power of mothering practices during my academic journey. Through personal narrative, this chapter will illuminate how mothering got me thru and made me a successful academic today, my mothers' roles during my academic experience, and lessons that are helpful to early career Black scholars or faculty that mentor Black students.

*Keywords:* Mothering; othermothering; antiblackness; refusal; relational

> The academy is not paradise. But learning is a place where paradise can be created. The classroom, with all its limitations, remains a location of possibility. (hooks, 1994, p. 207)

> …my mother tried to make a small path through the wake…she made livable moments, spaces, and places in the midst of all that was unlivable there…In other words, even as we experienced, recognized, and lived subjection, we did not *simply* or *only* live *in* subjection and *as* the subjected. (Sharpe, 2016, p. 4)

## THE ACCOMPLISHMENT OF THE INVISIBLE MAN: SURVIVING IT ALL

Since earning my PhD May 2019 from Washington State University (WSU), I have had many accomplishments—and they came fast. I landed a clinical professor position by that summer. A year later, I had transitioned into a tenure-track position at WSU. At the end of my first year on the tenure track, I became one of the Associate Deans in the College of Education. I was just re-appointed for another 2-year term in Summer 2023. I have accomplished all this between the COVID-19 pandemic, gratuitous state and white vigilante violence levied against Black communities, the 2020 uprisings, and right-wing advocates harnessing juridical-political power to intrude, curtail, and eliminate equity-oriented practices and academic freedom. Reflecting on all that I have done in 4 years is hard to encapsulate, because it is so bittersweet. I think the greatest accomplishment is surviving it all because academia is *no paradise* (hooks, 1994), but a battleground (Yancy, 2008) for Black men struggling to be a possibility. To be a Black scholar, you must always be triumphant against the lonely road of insurmountable odds. For instance, when I graduated with my PhD, the National Center for Science and Engineering Statistics (2020) reported that out of the total 2019 US citizen doctoral recipient population, 7% were Black. This abysmal trend extends to the academic hierarchies in the professoriate, as the National Center for Education Statistics (NCES) (2021) reported that only 2% of all tenured professors are Black. *Do Black men exist and/or matter in academia, and if so, where?* The data reminds Black (male) intellectuals of their spectral presence in this vast sea of institutional whiteness.

Despite commitments to racial inclusion, the realm of the "intellectual" at predominately white institutions (PWIs) is primarily reserved for white people (Puwar, 2004). PWIs are white spaces (Anderson, 2015) because the gathering, presence, and accumulation of white bodies, coinciding with Black bodies' absence, which contours spatial norms about belonging and exclusion. Bodies, spaces, and the imaginations of bodies in spaces are not neutral, as they are situated by shifting socio-historical constructions of race, gender, and ability (Puwar, 2004). These social dynamics exclude certain racialized people (e.g., Black men) from certain spaces and relegate them to others. Academia is not exempt from participating in this racialized exclusion but is *governed by it* (Ohito & Brown, 2021). The spatial illegitimacy of Black faculty and students within academia (Jenkins, 2021) is due to the entrenchment of antiblackness in higher education (Brooms & Druery, 2023; Dancy et al., 2018; Deckman, 2022; Dumas, 2016; Mustaffa, 2017; Ohito & Brown, 2021).

Situated by a cultural contempt for Blackness (Dumas, 2016), antiblackness is the "epistemic, ideological, material, and/or spiritual violence against Black people" (Ohito & Brown, 2021, p. 139). Foreclosed by *white ideas of Blackness* (Yancy, 2005), PWIs are a perpetual site of spatialized terror (Jenkins, 2021) as Black faculty and students are met with a myriad of violence that relegates them to academia's periphery. This violence, masked as normal (Mustaffa, 2017), distorts and forecloses Black epistemological ways of knowing, being, and relationality. This discursive and metaphorical violence was evident in the recent hashtag #BlackInTheIvory (Davis, 2021). Across disciplines and academic levels, the outpouring of tweets-as-vignettes illuminated Black faculty and students' precarity and the mundaneness of their violability. These violations denigrating Black intelligence, ability, and character, *phenomenologically return* (Yancy, 2005) the Black body as foreign unto itself. An apparition via representation and identity: *Academia is no paradise.*

Despite living in subjection and as the subjected (Sharpe, 2016), I *made it thru*. I traversed the sea of whiteness—not by neoliberal discourses of grit, determination, and rugged individualism—but by tapping into a radical Black relational ontology centered on matrilineal caregiving, critical care, radical love, communion, and institutional guardianship. My academic success is indebted to the significance of Black mothering, *othermothering* (Collins, 2000), and *further mothering* (Brockenbrough, 2014). Through Black feminist contexts (Collins, 2000), the concepts behind mothering and motherwork (Bernard et al., 2000) extend beyond birthmothers, as it was a survival mechanism to protect Black children's physical and emotional well-being (Bernard et al., 2012) from anti-Black violence. Mothering matters because it carves out space for Black humanity to not live in a permanent state of subjection. As such, mothering and motherwork remain a crucial practice within Black communities, and that importance is extended to universities as faculty took up that responsibility to meet students' holistic needs (Bernard et al., 2000). While Black mothering, othermothering, and further mothering do not dismantle oppression, its notions of caring, radical love, communion, and institutional guardianship create a *small wake* for Black students to traverse its *hazardous weather* (Sharpe, 2016). The love, care, labor, and support of my biological mother, PhD mentor, and PhD advisor ensured the academy was not always a site of subjection but one of lived Blackness (Ohito & Brown, 2021).

This chapter will explicate the power and importance of mothering practices during my academic journey and they have informed my scholarship.

Through personal narrative, this chapter will illuminate how mothering got me thru and made me as the academic today, my mothers' roles during my academic experience, and lessons that are helpful to early career Black scholars or faculty that mentor Black students. Proceeding from this section, I begin with a discussion of Black mothering, othermothering, and further mothering. From there, I share how mothering has informed my research. Finally, I provide academic advice to Black faculty and students so they can dream of themselves as possibilities beyond the structures imposed upon them.

## BLACK MOTHERING, OTHERMOTHERING, AND FURTHER MOTHERING: A DISCUSSION

Within the US, Black motherhood is a contradictory institution (Collins, 2000), as Black mothers are situated between being revered and reviled. They are essential to preserving Black life (Hartman, 2016; Smith, 2016) and historically pathologized for the Black family's destruction, deviancy, cultural inferiority, and Black men's social castration (Collins, 2000; Moynihan, 1968). Moreover, Black mothers are denied claims to womanhood and femininity (Spillers, 1987) by prevailing *controlling images* (Collins, 2000) in society. These contradictions extend to social-political thought as Black mothers and women's ideas are rendered opaque and peripheral to endeavors of Black resistance, refusal, and insurgency (Hartman, 2016), while simultaneously central to creating oppositional knowledge and challenging oppressions at the intersections of race, class, gender, sexuality, and nation (Collins, 2000). Within these contexts, Black mothers lived two lives: one for themselves and one for fellow Black women, Black communities, and Black children in their immediate and extended families (Collins, 2000). As such, they are constantly renegotiating the material conditions necessary for their existence within a racist hetero-patriarchal society (Smith, 2016) and devising new ways for their children to survive subjection.

*Who are Black children because of their mothers?* Hartman (2016) would answer, "Partus sequitur ventrem—the child follows the belly" (p. 166). During legalized enslavement, a Black mother's only right was to transfer her dispossession to the child (Hartman, 2016). As such, Black males are *indelibly marked by the Mother* (Spillers, 1987), inheriting a social world of subjection and placelessness. Denied paternal power, Spillers (1987) argued that Black males had the specific opportunity to learn from their mothers. By embracing Black maternal cultural knowledge, Black males could self-define their personhood (Spillers, 1987), resist and refuse oppressive systems (Collins, 2000), and negotiate their survival (Lorde, 1984). As nurturers and protectors, scholars have examined the complexities and maternal distress of Black mothers raisings Black sons in a world that views them as a social cancer (Davidson et al., 2016; Lorde, 1984; Mitchell & King, 1990; Smith, 2016). Black mothers face the daily dilemma of protecting Black boys from society's hostile forces and preparing to live in a vehemently violent anti-Black world. For mothers of Black sons, kinship remains an unstable social relation because it can be invaded by the capriciousness of anti-Black state-sponsored and vigilante violence (Smith, 2016; Spillers, 1987). Biological mothers cannot be everywhere to affirm their children's personhood; hence, othermothers are vital within Black communities.

## Othermothering

Collins (2000) defined othermothering as "women who assist bloodmothers by sharing mothering responsibilities" (p. 178). This cross-familial practice emerged during chattel slavery, as Black children were kinless by the sale or death of their mothers (Collins, 2000; Guiffrida, 2005; Hirt et al., 2008; Mawhinney, 2012). As fictive kin, othermothers' communal care ensured that Black children were physically and psychologically nurtured. Though slavery ended, othermothering did not, as Black children's maternal advocacy expanded into educational institutions (Bernard et al., 2012; Foster, 1993; Hirt et al., 2008; Mawhinney, 2012). At PWIs, othermothering is crucial to help Black students navigate academia's racially hostile white spaces (Anderson, 2015; Deckman, 2022). Black students have reported the difficulty of having positive faculty-student relationships (McCallum, 2020) because they must endure microaggressions from culturally insensitive white faculty who possess insular views about racism (Guiffrida, 2005). Othermothering was vital to Black students' intellectual welfare because Black women faculty's pedagogical practices went beyond traditional approaches of teaching and mentoring to ensure they succeed (Collins, 2000; Foster, 1993).

As a framework for Black student success, othermothering had three essential components: an ethic of care, cultural advancement, and institutional guardianship (Bernard et al., 2012; Hirt et al., 2008). An *ethic of care* refers to the emotional response attuned to Black students' political, social, and economic circumstances (Foster, 1993). Roseboro and Ross (2009) mentioned that this ethic of care is both "defensive and proactive, embodied and performed, private and public" (p. 21). *Cultural advancement* refers to the moral responsibility and vested interest in advancing Black students' lives from start to finish (Bernard et al., 2012; Hirt et al., 2008). Lastly, *institutional guardianship* refers to Black women faculty's transfer of Black cultural and intellectual capital to the next generation of Black scholars by maintaining high academic expectations (Bernard et al., 2012;

Hirt et al., 2008). Othermothering is a powerful, culturally responsive practice; however, the challenge is that Black women faculty are unavailable to many Black students. Between othermothering's high personal costs and the lack of Black women faculty in academia (NCES, 2021), Black students must ally with non-Black woman faculty to reach their academic and professional goals.

## Furthermothering

Brockenbrough (2014) stated that further mothering "attempts to mark white women educators' culturally responsive modes of maternal care for black youth" (p. 267). Despite white supremacy's entrenchment in education, some white women educators are unapologetic in loving, caring, and supporting Black students' educational endeavors. However, current academic literature would not situate these educators as othermothers because White women educators cannot directly embody Black women's matrilineal epistemologies regarding Black children's care and education. Inspired by Black women's othermothering practices, further, mothering is an additional layer of mothering for Black students. Brockenbrough (2014) highlighted five characteristics of further mothering: (1) critical interrogation of whiteness as power in an educator's identity and pedagogy, (2) possess a critical understanding of interlocking oppression that subjugates Black youth, (3) attempt to engage Black youth's cultures from their perspective, (4) acts of care, support, and advocacy must be meaningful to Black youth, and (5) Black youth must entrust the status to white women educators. Below are three vignettes about how my mothers' small paths in the wake shaped my positionality to be successful in academia.

## I AIN'T GETTING OFF THE BUS: A BLACK MOTHER'S STORY

All that I am is from my mother. My personhood comes from her. Through refusal, she taught me how not to live in subjection. Around eight years old, my mother took me and my brother on the bus to go shopping. After paying for us, the fare collector malfunctioned when she paid for herself. Accused of fare evasion, my mother refused to pay an additional fare, and the bus driver ceased bus service. *A crisis was created.* Some passengers became angry, and others offered to pay the fare, but my mother refused the choices offered; *she knew the truth*—she had paid the fare. She wasn't getting off the bus. The bus driver called the police, and they came to investigate. Eventually, the police demanded that the bus continue its operations.

Against the odds, my mother refused to give in to authority and have their personhood crushed by oppositional forces. We laugh about the story now, but I realized how influential that moment was. She challenged the mundane in a society where Black people are violently disciplined for questioning authority. Her refusal was less about us and more about what *she was unwilling to compromise for herself*. My mother's refusal taught me how to carve out space for my humanity without ceding to whiteness. As a Black scholar at a PWI, I constantly return to this story to meditate on what I am unwilling to compromise as an academic.

## AWW HELL-TO-THE-NO, THIS AIN'T IT: AN OTHERMOTHER STORY

Respect to my othermother, KCP (pseudonym). As my PhD mentor, KCP is why I attended my doctoral program and became a professor and administrator. KCP's aura was invigorating; she was an unapologetically Black woman professor. She had power, not over others, but to self-determine her world, boundaries, and margins. She had the power to challenge the mundane. *Keeping it real*, besides my mother, KCP was the only other person that could put the fear of God within me. She embodied institutional guardianship (Bernard et al., 2012). *Either come correct or do not come at all.* KCP was tough and had high expectations because she was preparing you to be a Black scholar. I never wanted to disappoint her because I knew how much she invested in my success, but one day I did. As a final paper for class, I wrote about Black masculinity and "coolness." I thought it was *the new hotness*, but *it was a two-pack of ass*. The paper was uncritical, the theories were grossly outdated, and I, as a Black man, did not talk about Black men in a robust, comprehensive way. My research read as if a white person wrote it. Her overall feedback was: *this ain't it*. Her refusal of my work generated a new path: one that humanizes and engenders ethical relationality with Black people at its nexus. Her feedback compelled me to meditate on my writing's purpose. *Who am I writing to/for, and why?* Initially, I thought the feedback was harsh, but I am grateful for it now. KCP's care about me and my research to say: *this ain't the way*. Now, as an institutional guardian, I share this story with my students as a mode of support and encouragement.

## IT'S ALL ABOUT RELATION: A FURTHER MOTHER STORY

*It's all about relation:* a phrase etched into my mind and lexicon. The legacy of completing a PhD program is having your PhD advisor as your inner voice. *It's all about relation*. From start to finish, CM (pseudonym) was vested in advancing my academic and professional goals. Yes, CM is a white woman, but she is a testament that further mothering exists in academia. She always interrogated her whiteness, and she understood the barriers I was up against. Sometimes, she was the barrier and knew when to give me space. CM was extraordinary because she was unapologetically there for me. CM was there when my dog died, when I won awards, when I got my tenure-track offer, when I castigated research, and when I wanted to quit. CM was there and still is. Her mentoring style did come at a personal cost: her academic career ambitions. CM sacrificed her career to advance the careers of her students. Refusing the dominant notions of rugged individualism that many academics praise, CM practiced communal care because *it's all about relation*. CM's mentoring style remains with me as I take on high service loads. The common discourse is saying no to service work. How can I rebuff service when I would not be successful without it? Moreover, how can I, as a Black scholar that writes about Black life, deny service to Black students? My scholarship would be disingenuous without my commitment to Black students. The personal cost is undoubtedly high, but what would Black communities be without sacrifice?

## REFUSING THE UNIVERSITY: A THEORETICAL WORD ON MY SCHOLARLY ACTIVITY

My scholarly activity on refusal is informed by the mothering that I received. Through refusal, I remain a Black possibility. Responsive to the needs of the now, refusal marks a limit and stoppage down a current path. It is a deliberate act of saying *we will continue this way no longer*. Refusal becomes a necessary intervention and improvisation to the metaphorical anti-Black violence that harms Black bodies. Deliberate, intentional, and willful (Simpson, 2016), refusal is a tactical repudiation of staying in lived objecthood. Based on the desire of *not-yet and not-anymore* (Tuck & Yang, 2014), refusal is generative (Simpson, 2016) because it forges new social relations, creating spaces for Black joy, life, and wonderment. Ultimately, desired-based refusal allows Black people to disrupt, intervene, evade, and heal amid all that is unlivable (Sharpe, 2016).

Tuck and Yang (2014) denoted how research remains a *dirty word* to minoritized people and communities because of settler colonialism's continuously-unfolding. As a scholar, your social world is structured around *the count*—the standard metrics needed for tenure. Criteria such as the number of journal publications, the nature of the outlet, its distribution (e.g., local, state, national, international), review process (referred vs. non-referred), and audience evaluate your progress toward tenure. Black scholars must acquiesce to metrics incongruent with their desires because they determine academic rigor and impact. I say *no thanks*. My research/publication pathway is untraditional by choice to dominant ways of "doing research." While some of my colleagues are unimpressed or underwhelmed by my publication outlets (e.g., book chapters, magazines), I refuse to decenter my desires. As a Black professor trained in Black Studies, my epistemological and methodological approaches to educational research and "knowledge production" are actively against the social and political matrix that organizes and orders white, western understandings of knowledge production (e.g., tenure). These dominant ways of producing "legible work" enact epistemic violence that limits Black capacities to "read, think, and imagine otherwise" (Sharpe, 2016, p. 13). Therefore, theorizing (and writing) about the specificity of (anti)Blackness will always unsettle epistemic, ontological, and axiological foundations of Western knowledge production. In a sense, I enjoy being undisciplined. What many would call "top-tier" journals are actively hostile and reductionist to (anti)Black specificity. What does rigor mean when I must contend with vigorous assaults against my body and intelligence? Why wait for post-tenure to publish in "low-brow" outlets when they are the community I write for? Writing about Blackness will never satisfy or fit the parameters imposed upon it. I write to expose the brutality of a system that many acquiesce to. I write to affirm that my research is *good enough* wherever it is submitted. I am unashamed for choosing publication outlets that engender ethical relationality with Black people at its nexus.

Being undisciplined, I would describe my scholarly activity as *fluid*. While my scholarship is centered on Black life, it is responsive to my interests. As such, I doubt I will be known as the scholar that does X or Y studies. Originally, my scholarship was focused the theoretical underpinnings of Black Boy Joy through Black aesthetics (see *The Joyful Sounds of Being Your Own Black Self*). COVID and the summer of racial reckoning happened, and my research shifted toward examining the aspatial nature of Black life due to antiblackness. Currently, I write about Black affect and thought from a lived embodied experience in an anti-Black world. It is truly challenging work because as a Black writer, I must describe this violence without being overwhelmed and disoriented by it. Writing about Black thought and feelings vis-à-vis antiblackness takes time, which is something that I am not always afforded. As I continue to grow in the profession, I cannot say where the trajectory of my works goes next, but I can tell that I will continue to *write what I like* and be unbashful about it.

## WHAT IS ONE THING YOU WISH YOU KNEW EARLY IN YOUR CAREER?

One thing that I wish I had known early in my career is that I am enough. My work is enough. Minoritized faculty and students at PWIs are susceptible to Western, colonial research logics and the proliferation of research productivity because of racialized power dynamics. Issa trap. I fell for it, too, and I constantly resisted/refused those logics as I continued to take up space in the academy. You can lose yourself and your goals chasing after what other people chase after. That mountain everyone is telling you to climb is simply a pile of rocks. Know that you do not have to do the dash because you are enough, already. Not many people in the academy will tell you that you are enough—that it is enough. Enough is seldom a viable phrase in scholars' vocabularies unless the phrase is not enough. The desire and infatuation to have more, to publish more, and keep the goalposts always on the move.

## WHAT ARE ONE OR TWO OPPORTUNITIES THAT WILL LEAD TO SUCCESS FOR A NEW FACULTY MEMBER?

The two opportunities that will lead to success are: attending conferences and using social media. Conferences can be expensive; however, they are worth it, especially early in your career. If you are on "the market" and presented with a job offer, please ensure to negotiate within your contract an allowance for research start-up funds and/or faculty research/professional development. Early career faculty should not "shoulder" the exorbitant costs of conference travel. Traveling to conferences allowed me to meet with Black education studies scholars and occupy a space with a Blackened consciousness and not be interrupted by white epistemologies. Moreover, attending conferences allowed me to see what is current in the field, what remains disputed, and what remains a possibility. It is an utter joy to attend conference sessions with scholars that read and admired as a graduate student. That joy deepens when you are a panelist with them during a conference session. If you are in the field of education, it is imperative that you attend the American Educational Research Association (AERA) and the American Educational Studies Association (AESA). Both organizations are fantastic at advancing your career through disseminating research, networking with like-minded scholars, and meeting with academic publishers.

Social media is another phenomenal tool that can advance your career. In my opinion, LinkedIn is a professional platform to formally connect with scholars in the field and find publication opportunities. In my opinion, I feel like you must have a LinkedIn profile to maintain a "scholarly image" because academia is very superficial about keeping up with appearances.

My favorite platform to use is Twitter/X (s/o to Black Twitter). Despite the increase of platforming hate and bigotry and ineptitude of management, I still see Twitter as a site of possibility because of the Black scholars that remain on it. Twitter introduced me to scholars I would have never met/read, perspective-widening conversations regarding Black social life, in real-time. Where else will you find that? In many ways, I see Black Twitter as an extension of that Blackened consciousness. Moreover, Twitter is a fantastic resource to find new and forthcoming scholarship, book recommendations for courses, foundational texts from Black authors, and publication opportunities. If you are not on Twitter, you are truly missing out.

## WHAT ARE FIVE TIPS FOR FACULTY SUCCESS IN HIGHER EDUCATION?

1. *Do not cede space to white epistemologies.* The wages of whiteness will gobble you up and distract you from the possibilities that you envision for yourself if you do not own your space and take up more when you can. Obviously, this is easier said than done, however, it is an important tip to practice. Create boundaries and enforce them. Be unforgiving at times about your principles. Be okay with refusing the status quo.
2. *If you can afford a therapist, get one.* In the academy, professors scoff at and laugh off therapy and mental health—it is truly *nasty work*. What you will find is that many scholars gritted out their PhDs. without unpacking their shit. Being a Black academic at a PWI "weathers" you in ways unimaginable because acts of racism are quite commonplace. Your ways of knowing and being are constantly invalidated and pushed to the margins by white empiricism. Black affect is simultaneously rendered as *unthinkable*, exorbitant and inappropriate. Some will be envious of your success and will want to put you in "your place." You will experience situations that will leave indelible marks upon you and that is why it is paramount to process yourself in relation to these moments. Therapy is not a value-neutral profession and there are racist therapists. Through a thorough search, I found a therapist that specialized in race-based trauma—and it has been transformative. Despite the cost, it is a relief to be in a space where your thoughts and feelings are not maligned as complaints. Therapy provides clarity to my experiences, which allows me to write from a lived embodied experience. If you are interested in finding a therapist and do not know where to start, I recommend checking out the folks in your area through psychologytoday.com.

3. *Know your audience.* As a scholar, whom do you want to be in relation with and why? Developing this answer is imperative to deciding your research endeavors. There are many scholars that write about Black people (e.g., inequalities, anti-Black pathologies) but are not in relation *with* Black people. That difference is important to recognize because one route will get you notoriety and the other requires a deep ethical commitment. The question comes down to who your audience is. I do not write for a universal audience, nor am I interested in doing so. I am a Black scholar that centers the sociality of Black life. Making this declaration is liberating because I do not have to "water-down" my content to make it palatable. Will my work bother some people? Surely, but they are not the audience that I am writing for. When you know who your audience is, you can quiet that external noise around and focus on your scholarship.
4. *Do not wait for tenure to do what you want to do.* Tenure is not a salve; it will not protect you from anti-Black violence. Hell, with the current political landscape of higher education, tenure may be gone. Senior scholars may advise you to wait until tenure to be "radical" with your scholarship. However, having tenure does not make you radical, it just makes you more of what you are. If you were *laying low* pre-tenure to avoid controversial topics, chances are you will be laying low after tenure. Moreover, Black people do not have the privilege to wait for the most opportune time to do anything. If Black people waited on the deliberate speed of institutions, where would we be? All that to say, write that publication you wanted. Take chances. Get involved. Challenge the status quo.
5. *Listen to your momma.* I am only here because of my mothers' love, support, care, and wisdom. Tap into the maternal knowledge that they provide you.

## REFERENCES

Anderson, E. (2015). The white space. *Sociology of Race and Ethnicity, 1*(1), 10 21. https://doi.org/10.1177/2332649214561306

Bernard, C., Bernard, W., Epko, C., Enang, J., Joseph, B., & Wane, N. (2000). "She Who Learns Teaches": Othermothering in the academy. *Journal of the Motherhood Initiative for Research and Community Involvement, 2*, 66–84.

Bernard, W. T., Issari, S., Moriah, J., Njiwaji, M., Obgan, P., & Tolliver, A. (2012). Othermothering in the academy: Using maternal advocacy for institutional change. *Journal of the Motherhood Initiative for Research and Community Involvement, 3*.

Brockenbrough, E. (2014). Further mothering: Reconceptualizing White women educators' work with Black youth. *Equity & Excellence in Education, 47*(3), 253–272. https://doi.org/10.1080/10665684.2014.933758

Brooms, D. R., & Druery, J. E. (2023). Between the world and us: Black men navigating antiblackness at historically white institutions. *Educational Studies*, 1–20. https://doi.org/10.1080/00131946.2023.2207696

Collins, P. H. (2000). *Black feminist thought: Knowledge, consciousness, and the politics of empowerment.* Routledge.

Dancy, T. E., Edwards, K. T., & Earl Davis, J. (2018). Historically white universities and plantation politics: Anti-blackness and higher education in the Black lives matter era. *Urban Education, 53*(2), 176–195. https://doi.org/10.1177/0042085918754328

Davidson, M. del G., Hadley, S., & Yancy, G. (2016). In M. del G. S. Davidson, S. J. Hadley, & G. Yancy (Eds.), *Our black sons matter: Mothers talk about fears, sorrows, and hopes.* Rowman & Littlefield.

Davis, S. M. (2021). The creator. *Black in the Ivory.* https://blackintheivory.net/creator

Deckman, S. L. (2022). *Black space: Negotiating race, diversity, and belonging in the ivory tower.* Rutgers University Press.

Dumas, M. J. (2016). Against the dark: Antiblackness in education policy and discourse. *Theory Into Practice, 55*(1), 11–19. https://doi.org/10.1080/00405841.2016.1116852

Foster, M. (1993). Othermothers: Exploring the educational philosophy of Black American women teachers. In M. Arnot & K. Weiler (Eds.), *Feminism and social justice in education: International perspectives* (pp. 101–123). Falmer Press.

Guiffrida, D. (2005). Othermothering as a framework for understanding African American students' definitions of student-centered faculty. *The Journal of Higher Education, 76*(6), 701–723. http://www.jstor.org/stable/3838783

Hartman, S. (2016). The belly of the world: A note on Black women's labors. *Souls, 18*(1), 166–173. http://doi.org/10.1080/10999949.2016.1162596

Hirt, J., Amelink, C., McFeeters, B., & Strayhorn, T. (2008). A system of othermothering: Student affairs administrators' perceptions of relationships with students at historically Black colleges. *Journal of Student Affairs Research and Practice, 45*(2), 382–408. https://doi.org/10.2202/1949-6605.1948

hooks, b. (1994). *Teaching to transgress: Education as the practice of freedom.* Taylor & Francis.

Jenkins, D. A. (2021). Unspoken grammar of place: Anti-Blackness as a spatial imaginary in education. *Journal of School Leadership, 31*(1–2), 107–126. https://doi.org/10.1177/1052684621992768

Mawhinney, L. (2012). Othermothering: A personal narrative exploring relationships between Black female faculty and students. *Negro Educational Review, 62–63*(1–4), 213–232.

McCallum, C. M. (2020). Othermothering: Exploring African American graduate students' decision to pursue the doctorate. *The Journal of Higher Education, 91*(6), 953–976. https://doi.org/10.1080/00221546.2020.1731262

Mitchell, C. A., & King, J. E. (1990). *Black mothers to sons: Juxtaposing African American literature with social practice.* P. Lang.

Moynihan, D. P. (1968). The culture of poverty. In D. Patrick Moynihan (Ed.), *On understanding poverty: Perspectives from the social sciences* (220, p. 187). Basic Books.

Mustaffa, J. B. (2017). Mapping violence, naming life: A history of anti-Black oppression in the higher education system. *International Journal of Qualitative Studies in Education, 30*(8), 711–727. https://doi.org/10.1080/09518398.2017.1350299

National Center for Science and Engineering Statistics. (2020). Doctorate recipients, by ethnicity, race, and citizenship status: 2010–19 [Table]. https://ncses.nsf.gov/pubs/nsf21308/data-tables

Ohito, E. O., & Brown, K. B. (2021). Feeling safe from the storm of anti-Blackness: Black affective networks and the im/possibility of safe classroom spaces in predominantly White institutions. *Curriculum Inquiry, 51*(1), 135–160. https://doi.org/10.1080/03626784.2020.1843966

Puwar, N. (2004). *Space invaders: Race, gender and bodies out of place*. Berg.

Roseboro, D. L., & Ross, S. N. (2009). Care-sickness: Black women educators, care theory, and a hermeneutic of suspicion. *Educational Foundations, 23*, 19–40.

Sharpe, C. (2016). *In the wake: On Blackness and being*. Duke University Press.

Simpson, A. (2016). Consent's revenge. *Cultural Anthropology, 31*(3), 326–333. https://doi.org/10.14506/ca31.3.02

Smith, C. A. (2016). Facing the dragon: Black mothering, sequelae, and gendered necropolitics in the Americas. *Transform Anthropology, 24*(1), 31–48. https://doi.org/10.1111/traa.12055

Spillers, H. J. (1987). Mama's baby, papa's maybe: An American grammar book. *Diacritics, 17*(2), 64–81. https://doi.org/10.2307/464747

Tuck, E., & Yang, K. W. (2014). R-Words: Refusing research. In D. Paris & M. T. Winn (Eds.), *Humanizing research: Decolonizing qualitative inquiry with youth and communities* (pp. 223–247). Sage Publications.

U.S. Department of Education, National Center for Education Statistics. (2021). Full-time faculty in degree-granting postsecondary institutions, by race/ethnicity, sex, and academic rank: Fall 2018, Fall 2019, and Fall 2020. https://nces.ed.gov/programs/digest/d21/tables/dt21_315.20.asp

Yancy, G. (2005). Whiteness and the return of the Black body. *The Journal of Speculative Philosophy, 19*(4), 215–241. www.jstor.org/stable/25670583

Yancy, G. (2008). *Black bodies, white gazes: The continuing significance of race*. Rowan & Littlefield.

CHAPTER 5

# AT YOUR SERVICE: BUILDING COMMUNITY AND PROFESSIONAL IDENTITY THROUGH SERVICE

Anne K. Weed
*Keuka College, USA*

## ABSTRACT

Today's faculty face increased expectations in all facets of their professional lives. Faced with tight budgets, larger class sizes, the impending enrollment cliff, and declining public support, institutions generally expect more from their faculty. Consequently, overworked faculty, particularly new-career faculty, are likely to meet service expectations with a sense of apprehension. However, service need not be the ever-ravenous hydra waiting outside the office door. Early in one's academic career, institutional service can provide valuable opportunities to gain knowledge about institutional culture and develop beneficial relationships with colleagues that will support a sense of belonging and increase job satisfaction. This chapter will highlight my experiences with service as well as the benefits from service. These benefits include identifying committees that align with an individual's interests, developing their leadership abilities, building community, and yielding important networking connections with campus decision-makers. Connection, camaraderie, and community: beyond meeting the third leg of the tenure stool, these three intangibles are the true rewards of service and keys to success in academia.

*Keywords:* Early-career; tenure; higher education; job satisfaction; college faculty; women faculty; faculty governance; leadership; professional relationships; late-career

## AT YOUR SERVICE: BUILDING COMMUNITY AND PROFESSIONAL IDENTITY THROUGH SERVICE

Today, faculty work more hours than ever before, and expectations for institutional service have increased as institutions face numerous challenges. New faculty, in particular, are likely to face burnout and feel overwhelmed by competing demands as they strive to earn tenure. Whereas campus service is often dreaded, these opportunities for collaboration with colleagues can lead to personal growth, the development of leadership skills, and job satisfaction. Early-career faculty will benefit from taking the initiative to serve on committees and taskforces which will introduce them to their campus culture and that align with their interests and values. In doing so, they will build their professional identity and create community.

Upon accepting an appointment to a tenure-track position after 4 years of teaching composition as an adjunct, I was eager to officially join the full-time faculty ranks and get straight to work in my new role. Whereas I was acquainted with some of the faculty in my division, I had only limited involvement in and understanding of the college's culture. Soon after my appointment and upon the recommendation of my division chair, I sought election to one of six standing faculty committees; thus began my journey of personal and professional growth through service. Over 25 years, I served on all but one of the standing committees and innumerable task forces or ad hoc committees. This work was key to my institutional success, for it helped to create my professional identity and a sense of fulfillment that complemented my love of teaching.

Whereas the professional literature tells new faculty to focus on developing their research agendas and honing teaching skills to achieve tenure, the role of institutional service is largely discussed as "career suicide" (Reed, 2008) or as an onerous burden "that has the potential to drain a junior faculty's energy with poor return" ("Serves you right," 2010). In the face of institutional constraints posed by tight budgets, the impending enrollment cliff, and declining public support, faculty responsibilities have increased significantly. Not surprisingly, then, overworked faculty are likely to meet service expectations with a sense of dread, fearful that service will interfere with research agendas or heavy teaching loads on the journey to tenure. Early-career faculty, in particular, are cautioned to "do the minimal amount necessary to be considered a good citizen but no more" (Fusarelli, 2020).

I wanted desperately to be a "good citizen," so I did not feel dread, but I was unsure about what constituted "the minimal amount necessary" or even the maximum. What became immediately apparent, however, was the high expectation for "internal service," defined here as service "related to faculty governance, faculty recruitment, evaluation and promotion, student admissions and scholarships, program supervision, development and marketing, internal awards, etc." (Guarino & Borden, 2017, p. 673). At my institution, a small independent liberal arts college where excellent teaching was most highly valued, and service was ranked equally with professional development, campus culture emphasized a volunteer ethic. Thus, in addition to my faculty governance committee work, I was soon involved in serving on faculty search committees, completing program assessment tasks, and developing marketing materials for my program to support admissions efforts. I jumped headlong into these new responsibilities, but not without a growing sense that maybe I was taking on too much.

New faculty are not alone in their worries that their campus service could obstruct their progress. Associate-level faculty may also face challenges in being promoted to full professor, given heavy service expectations. Kulp and colleagues (2022) point out that women and faculty of color especially struggle with service demands, for they are "expected to be the go-to sponsor of student organizations, to mentor students of color, or to serve on diversity committees" (p. 89). In my case, I was soon in demand for special (and multiple) taskforces on academic advising, diversity, and interfaith initiatives, several of which I served on throughout my faculty years. Some senior faculty, on the other hand, may eschew service and adopt a basic "check the box" attitude toward their job, drifting into a kind of semiretirement (Fleischman et al., 2022), thereby increasing pressure on early- and mid-career faculty to take on the bulk of service work.

With service so little regarded in the tenure and promotion process, why, then, do some faculty invest heavily in these activities, even at the risk of jeopardizing their acquiring tenure or impeding their promotion to full professor? Many faculty at all levels engage in service because they recognize that these commitments are essential to the health and success of the institution, for faculty, staff, and students alike. And, of course, significant differences exist among institutions and disciplines regarding expectations for scholarship, teaching, and service. Although research expectations have increased at my home institution, teaching is still the major criterion, and service remains very important. With these institutional service expectations, my division chair's early advice to join one of the faculty governance committees was warranted, as my previous adjunct status had precluded such involvement. Equally significant to me was the opportunity to work with my colleagues in my new status as one of them. Although I had attended the well-intentioned and moderately helpful new faculty orientation sessions preceding the start of the fall semester, I still felt like an outsider. The faculty in my division were supportive, but occupied with their own classes and personal lives. My sense of isolation was acute, especially as I lived some distance from campus and, therefore, had limited ability to participate in the local social opportunities. I knew that I would have to rely on my committee work to find workplace friends, allies, and mentors.

To be sure, I sometimes later questioned my decision to plunge immediately into committee work. I was often exhausted by the efforts to balance work activities with my home obligations of raising three young children. Committee work certainly cut into valuable time that could have been spent elsewhere, and research underscores the concern that women faculty can feel trapped, overwhelmed, and unsure how to decline assignments with impunity. However, this early commitment to service was beneficial in countless ways:

> Campus service participation can, nevertheless, support women faculty's career advancement when faculty use campus service to gain access to 'system knowledge,' which may otherwise be unavailable to them, such as enhanced access to budget information, names and faces of senior leaders, operating data, potential mentors and sponsors outside their unit, and peer allies and alliances. (O'Meara et al., 2017, p. 693)

This was true in my case, for I gained visibility outside of my division and began to build relationships with senior administrators and other decision-makers at the college, including faculty on the reappointment, promotion, and tenure committee. Most importantly, I began to feel connected to my academic "home," no longer the outsider looking in.

This feeling of belonging to my community was the result of a growing understanding of my college's unique culture. As an adjunct, I had perceived only dimly "the norms, values, practices, beliefs, and assumptions that shape the behavior of individuals and groups in a college or university" (Kuh & Whitt, 1988, p. 6). Consequently, I had marginal knowledge of how experiential learning, encapsulated as Field Period, was central to its identity and guided institutional policymaking. I had not understood how the composition of our student body, with a sizable number of first-generation students and nearly all students receiving significant financial aid, influenced resource allocation and pedagogical initiatives. With my election to the Faculty Development Committee, I was introduced to both the formal and informal culture of the college, its stories, its challenges, and its sources of pride.

I was fortunate to have this early introduction to service. During those first 3 years on the Faculty Development Committee, I worked with senior colleagues who introduced me to institutional norms and served as informal mentors who encouraged me to share my ideas and concerns about teaching and learning in a safe environment. Through our collective work on policy development, review of faculty grant requests, creation of teaching resources, and hosting ongoing pedagogy workshops, I gained new insights into how to improve my teaching, and my knowledge of the inner workings of the college expanded. So too did my sense of self-efficacy, both within the classroom and within the college community, for I saw that my contributions were valued and respected by senior faculty members, an important aspect of newcomer adjustment (Ponjuan et al., 2011). And I developed deeply satisfying professional relationships that provided personal and professional support. Twenty years later, these relationships continue to nurture and sustain me.

The early rewards of service engagement—connections to my colleagues and a sense of belonging—were augmented by personal growth as I became more confident with institutional decision-making. As I reflected on my service work during annual self-evaluations, I felt a strong sense of congruency (my work aligned with the mission and vision of the college), agency (my work had impact on the college's operations), and an enhanced sense of professional identity and purpose (my work aligned with my beliefs and values of sharing expertise, responsibility, collaborating, and promoting the greater good of the institution).

Continued participation in shared governance committees, i.e., in matters of instructional policy, curriculum, general education, and promotion and tenure, supported the development of my emotional intelligence as well. Exposure to diverse perspectives, disagreements, and challenging interactions made me more attuned to my own emotional responses, helped me to take into account the emotions and concerns of others, and developed stronger emotional regulation skills. I grew to recognize those emotional triggers which interfered with clear thinking and to address patterns of behavior that impeded successful resolutions. For example, when I led the task force to revise the first-year seminar, our initial efforts to ramp up course outcomes and credits were met by some with anxiety, cynicism, and outright resistance. At base, these negative reactions were rooted in the fear that credit swapping would remove other courses in the general education curriculum, possibly their courses, and thereby threaten their institutional status quo and job security. By directing and maintaining focus on the common good—the benefit to students of an improved course and to the college of increased freshmen retention—and by listening empathetically and demonstrating respect for those asking hard questions, we were able to identify solutions.

Committee service also provides valuable training in practical skills. Jafar et al. (2017) provide a useful summary:

> When faculty participate in governance they learn skills that are often different from their disciplinary training: they gain organizational and administrative experience (for example, by learning how to run meetings effectively and how to develop an agenda); they develop mentoring skills as they expand their capacities to be attuned to the experiences and perspectives of others; they learn to work together to reach consensus through compromise, and they learn when to hold their ground; they practice negotiation and public speaking skills; and they learn the intricacies of parliamentary procedures, Robert's rules of order, and how to write motions and argue effectively for them. (para. 17)

This training also supported my pedagogical growth; many of these skills applied to the classroom and my interactions with students, from learning how to hold productive conferences with writing students, mentoring advisees through career planning, instructing students how to work effectively in groups for team projects, and even how to conduct debates on controversial topics as part of their research projects.

My service engagement increasingly brought me into contact with leadership opportunities where such practical foregrounding proved to be immensely helpful. A year after being tenured, I was elected chair of the division, with oversight of five academic programs, and 3 years later, in an unexpected career shift, I was appointed vice president for academic affairs. Through service on various standing and ad hoc committees, I had gained insight into institutional policies, educational standards, accreditation regulations, curriculum procedures, budget allocations, promotion and tenure policies, and college priorities, such as enrollment, retention, and diversity initiatives, among others. I still faced a very steep learning curve upon assuming the role of chief academic officer, but I felt competent addressing most, if not all, of the new responsibilities.

Upon returning to a faculty role after 5 years in administration, I readily resumed my committee service. Because late-career faculty members have a wealth of experience, knowledge, and institutional history, their continuation in faculty governance can be invaluable (Baldwin & Zeig, 2013). However, as a senior faculty member, I could have easily declined faculty nominations or administrative requests with a "been there, done that," or "time for other folks to step forward" response. Yet, my "good citizen" pathway had yielded high career satisfaction. For me, it was a joy to return to teaching AND to reconnect by working with colleagues from different departments on issues that mattered to the faculty and to the institution. I found myself reenergized by the opportunities to shape the direction and policies of the institution, especially those that advanced faculty interests. These included clarifying the promotion and tenure process, revising the post-tenure review process, and devising clock-stopping policies for pre-tenure track faculty. I am grateful to have had the opportunity to make contributions that will have a lasting and positive impact. I also valued the intellectual stimulation presented by new initiatives and ideas beyond my regular teaching, such as strengthening academic advising and addressing the pedagogical challenges posed by generative AI chatbots. In short, continued service work kept me engaged, informed, fulfilled, and vitally involved in the success of the college.

## PROUDEST ACCOMPLISHMENT

Two years after promotion to associate professor, I was awarded the college's most prestigious award, Professor of the Year. Candidates are nominated by faculty, including division chairs, and the recipient is selected by a faculty group in concert with the provost, student trustees, and president. Per the college *Faculty Handbook*, the award is based on "excellent performance in the classroom and excellent performance in other Faculty activities." Whereas my student end-of-course evaluations had been routinely very strong, my institutional service engagement far outshone my scholarly activity, so the award was quite unexpected. When the award was announced at the spring commencement, the president extolled my positive influence on the lives and careers of my students and praised my service work for contributing to the improvement of the college. It was very gratifying to see that my colleagues and institutional leaders valued my contributions to the success of the college. The award also served as a tremendous motivation to continue my service engagement. Despite the "extra work," I have never regretted the direction my career took.

## THEORETICAL ALIGNMENT

My scholarly activities, focused on challenging patriarchal attitudes embodied in 19-century American novels, employed a feminist approach. This approach informed my teaching of a first-year course on argumentative writing, a cornerstone of my teaching career, in which we focused on issues of power, identity, and social inequities in classroom discussions and in writing assignments. Feminist pedagogy, with its focus on empowering students for the purpose of improving people's lives and achieving social justice, was especially relevant at my institution with its large population of first-generation and low-income students. My campus service participation also aligned well with my feminist values of learning with and from my colleagues as we worked collaboratively to improve the institution's operations, policies, and practices.

## WHAT I WISH I HAD KNOWN: BUILD (YOUR) COMMUNITY FROM DAY ONE

Because departments and colleges differ in their expectations for research, teaching, and service, because requirements for tenure and promotion can be vague or unclear, because it can be isolating when you make the transition to a new campus—you need to exercise agency in reaching out to individuals in your department and across campus to have conversations. Admittedly, initiating these conversations about your teaching, research, and service can be very intimidating since your colleagues have myriad responsibilities as well. I wish I had known that senior faculty, instead of being crusty curmudgeons, are eager to share their stories about working with students and their campus work. I thought they would be uninterested in the newcomer or too busy to meet over coffee or lunch. I hesitated, at first, to seek out and socialize with my committee colleagues, naively waiting for them to make such overtures. Moving into the uncomfortable direction of starting conversations with these well-respected seniors was the first step in developing a sense of belonging—and forming lifelong friendships. These conversations will identify avenues to meet service expectations in ways that align with your values and support your learning and growth. O'Meara and colleagues (2008) point out the value of building community, emphasizing "faculty learn, grow, and make contributions through professional relationships embedded in communities" (p. 166).

## OPPORTUNITIES THAT LEAD TO SUCCESS

When possible, participate in leadership development activities at your institution. These opportunities may come in the form of lunch-bag meetings, shared faculty readings, or formal institutional development programs open to all faculty and staff. This recommendation may seem to be adding a huge task to an already overwhelming agenda, but the rewards are multiple. Leadership skills translate well to the classroom and support academic advising relationships, assist you in meetings with your department chair or other supervisors, develop your sense of confidence and self-efficacy, and prepare you to assume leading roles in a variety of activities. Also important, your participation in campus leadership training activities will introduce you to other members of the academic and professional staff who will be invaluable to your success at the institution: registrar, student affairs professionals, financial aid and admissions officers, marketing and communication staff, etc. Relationships with these individuals will yield a greater understanding of the mutual dependency of all these institutional roles, awareness of the constraints and needs they face, and help you to create allies among these offices. These leadership skills are also valued in your local community, particularly parent-teacher organizations, and local school boards where individuals with deep knowledge of the postsecondary environment can support worthy K-12 educational initiatives. Lastly, participation in leadership development activities will grow your sense of optimism; inherent in such training is a belief in self-improvement, self-empowerment, and self-actualization.

## FIVE TIPS FOR FACULTY SUCCESS

1. *Attend in-house faculty workshops designed to enhance teaching effectiveness, even if you feel comfortable with your teaching skills.* Your attendance will be appreciated by the individuals leading the workshop, connect you with your colleagues, underscore your commitment to growth by the administration, and best of all, provide you with at least one new idea that can keep alive your passion for teaching. Moreover, in-house professional development workshops often reflect changing institutional priorities and directions, such as how to modify assignments in the face of AI challenges, so attendance can indicate your willingness to move into new areas of concern or promise for the institution.
2. *Introduce yourself to and work with the educational technology team on campus.* This team may include educational technologists, IT staff, instructional designers, and other faculty, all of whom are exploring and developing ways to use technological innovations to support and improve student learning outcomes. This group can keep you apprised of new tools available to faculty, provide encouragement and support, and model how to use them effectively.
3. *Read your institution's most recent accreditation report,* when you have a couple of spare hours. Faculty involvement in the accreditation process is crucial to institutional success, but most new faculty—and often current faculty—have a limited understanding of accreditation processes. For new faculty, the accreditation report provides valuable information about how well an institution meets the accreditors' standards, typically organized by the following categories: mission, institutional integrity, the student learning experience and support for students, assessment of educational effectiveness, institutional planning and financial resources, and governance/leadership. This report will provide the clearest and most comprehensive picture of the challenges and opportunities your institution faces, as well as a perspective on the things that matter most. Your knowledge of your new academic "home" will grow exponentially.

4. *Eat regularly in the student dining hall and faculty dining hall.* It will be good for your students to see you in their space, you can commiserate about the quality of the food, you can join them and continue conversations begun in class, or you can find the student who has been AWOL from your class. In the faculty dining hall, your presence is noted, and you can start those informal conversations to start building your community. I did not do this often enough. As a new faculty member, I thought it was better to save some dollars and get more work done, but in hindsight, I rarely got much done in that "extra" hour.
5. *Lastly, take a daily or weekly walk with other faculty and/or staff,* even if only a half hour. Your physical and mental health will benefit, and you will find a new source of camaraderie.

## REFERENCES

Baldwin, R. G., & Zeig, M. J. (2013, May 10). The potential of late-career professors. *Inside Higher Ed.* https://www.insidehighered.com/advice/2013/05/10/tapping-potential-late-career-professors-essay

Fleischman, G., Oler, D., & Skousen, C. J. (2022). Advice for senior faculty: Supporting and building your school. *SSRN.* http://doi.org/10.2139/ssrn.3944001

Fusarelli, L. D. (2020, August 5). If I only knew: Reflections for new faculty members. *Inside Higher Ed.* https://www.insidehighered.com/advice/2020/08/06/seasoned-faculty-member-reflects-what-he-wishes-hed-known-new-professor-opinion

Guarino, C. M., & Borden, V. M. H. (2017). Faculty service loads and gender: Are women taking care of the academic family? *Research in Higher Education, 58,* 672–694. http://doi.org/10.1007/s11162-017-9454-2

*Inside Higher Ed.* (2010, June 17). Serves you right. *Inside Higher Ed.* https://www.insidehighered.com/advice/2010/06/18/serves-you-right

Jafar, A., Feldman, S., & Chrisler, J. C. (2017). Hang together or hang separately: The importance of participating in governance on small campuses. *Academe.* https://www.aaup.org/article/hang-together-or-hang-separately

Kuh, G. D., & Whitt, E. J. (1988). The invisible tapestry: Culture in American colleges and universities. *ASHE-ERIC Higher Education Report, 1.*

Kulp, A. M., Pascale, A. B., & Wolf-Wendel, L. (2022). Clear as mud: Promotion clarity by gender and BIPOC status across the associate professor lifespan. *Innovative Higher Education, 47,* 73–94. https://doi.org/10.1007/s10755-021-09565-7

O'Meara, K. A., Kuvaeva, A., & Nyunt, G. (2017). Constrained choices: A view of campus service inequality from annual faculty reports. *The Journal of Higher Education, 88*(5), 672–700. http://doi.org/10.1080/00221546.2016.1257312

O'Meara, K. A., Terosky, A. L., & Neumann, A. (2008). Faculty careers and work lives: A professional growth perspective. *ASHE Higher Education Report, 34.*

Ponjuan, L., Conley, V. M., & Trower, C. (2011). Career stage differences in pretenure track faculty perceptions of professional and personal relationships with colleagues. *The Journal of Higher Education*, *82*(3), 319–346. https://doi.org/10.1353/jhe.2011.0015

Reed, M. [Dean dad] (2008, July 27). Confessions of a community college dean: Thoughts on service. *Inside Higher Ed*. https://www.insidehighered.com/blogs/confessions-community-college-dean/thoughts-service

# SECTION 2

I CAN'T DO THIS ON MY OWN, YOU CAN'T EITHER

CHAPTER 6

# EXPERIENCES AND MENTORING NEEDS OF A NEW INTERNATIONAL COUNSELOR EDUCATOR IN THE US

**Suelle Micallef Marmara**
*University of Wisonsin River-Falls, USA*

### ABSTRACT

The counseling profession is becoming globalized more than ever, leading to more counselors seeking to pursue graduate studies in counseling in the United States. This leads to more counselors holding a doctorate wishing to secure faculty positions in the US as counselor educators. This chapter will highlight an international counselor educator's experiences and mentoring needs in a US counselor education faculty position. It will present some cultural challenges faced at different stages of the counselor-educator process, including initial adjustment to a faculty position and the mentoring needs in teaching, scholarly, and service work.

*Keywords:* International faculty; new faculty; mentoring; success tips; acceptance

## MY STORY AS A NEW INTERNATIONAL FACULTY

New experiences present opportunities to grow and develop in many areas. My experiences began by moving away from my family 4 years ago to pursue my doctorate. Then, within 3 years, I moved away from my friends who became my family, to embark on a new career in higher education in a different state. This new journey has demanded personal and professional changes and transitions. As soon as I started my new position as an assistant professor, my primary goal was to learn about the program and get to know my colleagues and other stakeholders who significantly contribute to this program. My goal was to immerse myself in the culture and broaden my worldview, as I believed it would help me to improve communication, build stronger relationships, reduce conflict, and increase empathy while navigating the new experiences. Thus, I engaged in various activities within the university and the community, such as biking, skiing, attending fairs, and socializing with people born and raised here. Learning about the culture, standard practices, and different worldviews of different people enriched my personal growth and fostered deeper connections with colleagues and students. This helped me tailor my communication and teaching style to be sensitive to students' different needs. Additionally, I could navigate any possible misunderstandings more effectively through cultural awareness.

Overall, my biggest challenge was time management. With this, I struggled to accomplish my fourth and fifth goals, i.e., service and scholarly activity. I was glad my team supported me in postponing my total involvement in my service responsibilities to my second year and for my first year to prioritize learning my role and expectations. Regarding my scholarly activity, although I had a clear research agenda navigating the publication system in the US took a lot of work. The academic publication process varies in different countries. Thus, I had to identify which journals are most relevant to my work and learn about the impact factor, readership, and types of articles colleagues typically publish. So yes, as it may sound like a lot, that is how it felt! It was challenging to navigate multiple things within academia while adjusting to the cultural transition, and dealing with loneliness, social isolation, and homesickness. While I acknowledge that my first year has been, at times, an overwhelming and challenging year, yet through the support, guidance, and mentorship I managed to accomplish my responsibilities in all three areas of evaluation (teaching, scholarly activity, and service) to different extents. Having mentors I can contact for guidance was crucial to my success.

## ACADEMIC-RELATED ACCOMPLISHMENT

Teaching has been my most successful area this year. One of my strengths is my ability to work collaboratively, so I enjoyed successfully co-teaching courses during my first year. Looking back, I am thankful for Dr Kemer (doctorate studies advisor) advising me to advocate for myself during the job offer negotiations. I requested one class release each semester for my first year to help me navigate the challenges of adjusting to the different transitions of the move and starting a new career. This led to an alternative offer to co-teach two classes rather than an entire class release each semester. Being allowed to co-teach two and independently teach one class during both semesters of my first year as a new faculty was considerable support. During my co-teaching experiences, I had the opportunity to learn more about my colleagues' different teaching styles and methods and learn more about the program. Working closely with my team also helped me ensure my course assignments and tasks aligned with the Council for Accreditation of Counseling and Related Educational Programs (CACREP) standards requirements and the program, specifically, those I was teaching independently.

Another academic accomplishment I was proud to have achieved by the end of my first year as an assistant professor was submitting a manuscript from my dissertation for possible publication in a counseling journal and presenting at the American Counseling Association conference. Since my position is within a teaching-focused university, the faculty mentoring support was primarily focused on teaching and adjusting to the system with minimal reliance on how I could start my scholarly activity. Feeling isolated and at a loss in my research and writing activity did not help my self-discipline in writing. However, connecting back with my dissertation chair for scholarly mentoring and attending a training workshop at the university to support faculty in writing techniques helped boost my motivation to narrow my research agenda to monthly reachable goals.

Moreover, what helped my motivation to start working in my scholarly area were the visits of some faculty members within and outside of my department. They showed interest in how I was doing and provided me with guidance and opportunities to grow my scholarly activities. This support led me to be more intentional in prioritizing writing, identifying what to write about, and what work I already have that can be changed into a manuscript submission. I learned that I do not need to reinvent the wheel but invest time in projects I had already started during my doctorate.

**Theories that align with My Scholarly Work.** Various successful elements in my first year were developed from fostering active collaboration with colleagues and students in all my classes. I had to learn to be comfortable being vulnerable and open with colleagues and students when I did not know something or could not answer a question posed. My teaching philosophy is driven by the student-centered constructivist approach of McAuliffe and Eriksen (2011) and Jane Vellas' (2002) adult learning and education principles. These theories helped me in my classroom, as they allowed me to move away from the expert position and engaged in learning with the students. Through open conversations and class discussions with students, we build new knowledge. I observed that not taking the expert position in the classroom helped me release the pressure of perfection while creating a safe and constructive atmosphere in the classroom. It promoted a positive learning attitude where students allowed themselves to be vulnerable, share their concerns, apprehensions, and views, and be who they are. I appreciated each student holistically and valued everything that each student brought to the learning process. During all my classes, students were engaged, enthusiastic to learn, and felt safe to express confusion, misunderstanding, and conflict. Additionally, my research philosophy of social constructivism supported me to work with two other assistant professors in exploring and discussing the ethical standards for post-COVID-19. Using a social constructivist research theory, we devised and presented the topic at the American Counseling Association conference.

## CHALLENGES, MENTORING SUPPORT AND OPPORTUNITIES TO GROW

As a new international faculty member, working in a predominantly white institution with no other foreigners poses various challenges that add to the possible challenges faced by other new faculty members. By navigating through the latest systems and learning how things are done at the university, college, and department levels, I was trying to find my voice and develop a sense of belonging where my input is valued. My initial responsibility was to learn the system in place and then start sharing thoughts and opinions. However, seeing how shadowy some treated me, I was disheartened. Despite several faculty members showing interest in hearing how I was doing, when it came to my ideas, I often felt I needed to be more recognized by my identity as an international and new faculty. Their response to my ideas/opinions or suggestions were, "I appreciate your reflections and taking the time, but...." "It's a good idea, but this has worked well for many years" or "in the states...." I started feeling like a novice in counseling, even though I had been practicing for over ten years and had a strong identity as a school and clinical counselor. I felt my views were in the conversations, but only some faculty members' voices were considered when making decisions. It felt like being molded into becoming who they wanted me to be and losing my identity as a counselor and supervisor. This made me feel less than others and that my voice did not matter. I then started to feel like an "alien" just like the label given to me by the US government.

Conversely, my biggest challenge to finding my voice within the team was facing the "imposter syndrome." I often doubted myself and felt incompetent next to other faculty members born in this country and have been in academia for over fifteen years with several publications. I dismissed my achievements and experiences in the counseling field by comparing myself to the academic work my colleague had achieved. I valued my colleagues' ethnicity as their primary right to have a voice and to finalize decisions and dismissed my right to voice things out. I felt different and isolated, hindering my sense of belonging within a supportive environment.

Although I worked in a supportive, welcoming, and accepting environment within a predominantly white American citizen institution, I felt unsafe processing my irrational self-doubt. I feared being misinterpreted or misunderstood. I would have loved to connect with other international faculty members and share my thoughts and insecurities, but I prioritized work and dismissed my personal needs. Often, I needed that extra push to convince myself that although I am an "alien," I earned this space, and my voice and working experiences in my country count. I had to ground myself and connect with who I am and my experience in counseling to support me in finding ways to be myself within a foreign space. However, having an open conversation with my colleagues about their expectations and periodically asking for feedback on my performance gave me the clarity and the reassurance I needed. Talking about my fears and insecurities with other new faculty members out of my department and my mentors, Dr Lee and Dr Kemer, out of the university, helped me realize what I felt was common and that I earned my place, giving me the same rights to have a voice. Additionally, having a supportive mentor Dr Baker within my program, with whom I felt comfortable being emotionally vulnerable, helped me to believe in myself and challenge myself to make my voice heard.

Another internal challenge I faced as a new faculty member was balancing life and work. No matter how much I worked, there was always more to do. I felt guilty enjoying some free alone time and family time because I should have been reading new articles and books on my research area, I should have been brainstorming new pedagogical methods, or improving my courses. I should have been researching for training offered by the university on teaching courses etc. Coming from a culture where perfection is rewarded and good enough is not valued, I often found myself over-preparing and spending more time on a task or lesson plan than was necessary for fear that my work wasn't good enough. It took some time until I learned to pull back and examine my expectations. Through open conversations with my program chair and mentor, I learned to permit myself to do "well enough" and acknowledge that my work was good enough for the students and my tenure track progression. While admitting that it was not easy to expose my vulnerability to my mentor, who was also the program chair, owning the power over my tenure track process, I believe that their support and understanding allowed me to be compassionate with myself. I challenged the internal pressure that I needed to show strength in all three areas (teaching, scholar, and service) within my first year. It allowed me to narrow my goals and work on my time management.

I devised a realistic, reachable plan to help me navigate my time. Considering that my biggest challenge was to integrate my scholarly activities within my other daily responsibilities, I planned to start my days with an hour of writing before moving on to prep for class, answering emails, holding office hours, and so on. The goal was to start to write when my brain was freshest, before, I felt worn out with all the other planned and unplanned activities of the day. Then I picked other days of the week to which I dedicated more than an hour to be more productive in my scholarly activity and reach my monthly writing goals. This experience taught me the importance of picking what's most essential and doing that before I get worn out. It also taught me to be disciplined about my research and teaching productivity as an ongoing commitment. Additionally, I learned the importance of adopting and being consistent in productive habits that foster work and life balance. Yet, up until today, I still struggle to put this plan into action and keep the balance. But I choose to be compassionate with myself and acknowledge my efforts, which is a work in progress.

## WHAT I WISHED I KNEW EARLY

The one thing I wished I had known before I embarked on this journey was to remind myself to honor who I am and all my accomplishments that led to acquiring the position of an assistant professor. Never feel less than yourself because you come from a different country than others and are new. I wish I knew and reminded myself that my voice matters no matter what.

I wish I knew the importance of being compassionate with myself by acknowledging that transitions into a new country and a new career bring about enormous challenges for everyone, and, naturally, one takes time to learn how to balance work and life. I took the advice of my external mentor Dr Lee that success in academia and life happiness are large products of good time management. Thus, I started focusing on getting enough done without working over 60 hours a week but started working smarter and not more extended hours. I devised a working budget by treating my job as a job, not my whole life. With flexible hours, it is easy to fall into the trap of mashing the work into your personal life. Instead, I think I was still in the mindset of being a doctorate student, where my studies are part of my personal life since they are personal accomplishments. Therefore, I started working on dividing the two by being more self-disciplined and focusing on my new mantra, "Good is good enough, and perfection doesn't exist."

All these confirmations and reminders would have helped my sense of self and belonging within my department. I would have felt more confident in my teaching leading to less anxiety and a more enjoyable experience. With less anxiety and self-doubt, I would have been open to my creativity.

I am a creative person who uses the present moment as an inspiration to create and provide what is needed there and then and within the here and now. Yet, through my self-doubt, I found myself too much in my head, with moments of blankness, questioning everything I knew with negative judgment, and not feeling good in my own skin. Believing that I own the right to have a space to be who I am within the team and in my classrooms would have supported me to share more of my clinical and school experiences with students and colleagues and provide different views and practices done from the US. Additionally, self-acceptance of being who I am in a foreign country would have assisted me in appreciating all my hard work and given me more permission to enjoy some free time. Consequently, this would have allowed me to rest and nourish myself, leading to more energy, less brain fog, and more productivity in a shorter period.

## SUGGESTIONS AS A MENTOR

Simply having diversity within a team does not automatically equate to an inclusive and supportive environment. I believe that diversity and inclusion are related yet distinct concepts that require separate attention. Therefore as faculty members supporting new international faculty, I would not only acknowledge the diverse representation of the new faculty member from the rest of the team but also focus on inclusion. I would look into how they are integrated and valued within the team and the university. I would put effort into listening to their needs that support their feelings of belonging while ensuring they are respected in their unique, different ways.

I would guide the new faculty to connect with other foreign faculty or provide them with the services available within the university that supports international faculty. It is essential to acknowledge the cultural transition that one is going through and, while helping them to learn how the system works, be also interested to know how it works in their country. Be open to including them and what they can bring as part of the new team. I would support the new faculty to advocate for themselves and what they represent by voicing their point of view and ideas even if they are shut down. This includes establishing a solid sense of self by acknowledging your accomplishments, advocating for yourself, and voicing what you stand for, which will support a better sense of belonging within the team and in one's career.

As a mentor of a new international faculty member, I would support the new faculty in building relationships with other colleagues by creating opportunities for social gatherings outside of the university. Creating activities between colleagues outside the department helps people get to know each other beyond academia. It also helps diminish the isolation experienced by new faculty members trying to find a sense of belonging.

Data obtained through a focus group from a study done by Phillips et al. (2016) indicated that for both minority and international faculty members, isolation was a significant contributor to job dissatisfaction. Therefore, creating opportunities for social networking outside of academia can assist the new international faculty in building relationships and create a space to feel comfortable reaching out with difficulties, challenges, or apprehensions. I encourage the new faculty to make time for social connections and activities. If they are not offered within one's department or college, one can join others that might be provided within the university.

## TIPS FOR FACULTY SUCCESS IN HIGHER EDUCATION

During my first year as an international new faculty member, I learned various things while navigating the challenges. Based on my experience, I came up with tips to support international faculty success in higher education.

1. *Understand that you are never finished working.* In academia, there is always worthwhile work you can do, and at the end of the day, you are never finished. Therefore, good time management, creating a productive time budget system, self-discipline, and treating your academic work as a job with a working window during the day will help you create a good work/life balance. You may need to challenge the notion that academia is a "calling" to avoid burning out.
2. *Be productive and not just busy.* For me, this means spending my most productive hours (mornings) on what is most important first and leaving the remaining time when I tend to be less focused on the less important things for my success in academia. This means starting the day with writing or teaching work and leave responding to emails and meetings for a later time during the day. Good time management and saying no when your plate is full will help you take care of yourself while working to your best.
3. *Know the criteria for retention, tenure, and promotion.* From the first day of your employment review the criteria for retention, tenure, and merit/annual review. You need to know what you do not know. Start an open conversation with your university mentor or program chair to gain a clear idea of all the criteria. A good understanding of what is expected from you supports your mental and emotional well-being as it will remove uncertainties that lead to stress and anxiety associated with the ambiguity of your role. Additionally, knowing what is expected from you provides a roadmap for your career development where you can start devising a specific, timely, and reachable plan to guarantee you will reach the expectation by the end of the year.

4. *Take care of yourself.* Do things that you enjoy and that nourish you. Invest time in staying connected with who you are, with your family in your country, and with the family that joined you in this transition. Build new connections and friendships outside of academia too. Focus on healthy nutrition and fitness because it will be easier to look at challenges from a positive rather than defeating perspective if you feel good in your body and mind. Seek counseling support or a trusted friend to process your thoughts, confusion, and cultural challenges. Do not ignore the emotional burden you are experiencing from all the new transitions by prioritizing work because, in the end, your work performance will still suffer. Thus, invest in your general well-being now, as it will reflect in your health and future academic success.
5. *Utilize mentoring.* If you are assigned a mentor in your department, use this resource to support your success. However, if you have a good relationship with a former mentor, I suggest contacting your former mentor for additional support. It is essential to have an external person with whom you feel safe to share challenges you fear sharing with the university mentor due to a conflict of interest. It is also beneficial to receive feedback and guidance from an outside person because they are not part of the group dynamics, so their perspective will be more neutral and less biased.
6. *Go beyond the walls of your university.* Learning what's beyond your university is essential. Therefore, I suggest attending and presenting at professional conferences. These will increase your opportunities to network professionally, get to know people, and be known. This will also open opportunities to work with other professionals on common research interests, share teaching tips, etc. Remember that your university can often cover travel expenses, so contact your department chair and investigate what is available for financial support.

## REFERENCES

McAuliffe, G., & Eriksen, K. (2011). *Handbook of counselor preparation: Constructivist, developmental, and experiential approaches.* Sage Publication.

Phillips, S. L., Dennison, S. T., & Davenport, M. A. (2016) High retention of minority and international faculty through a formal monitoring program. *To Improve the Academia: A Journal of Educational Development, 35*(1), 153–179. https://doi.org/10.1002/tia2.20034

Vella, J. (2002). *Learning to listen, learning to teach: The power of dialogue in educating adults.* Jossey-Bass.

CHAPTER 7

# A BIT OF ADVICE FOR EARLY CAREER FACULTY

**Karen R. Tellez-Chaires**
*California State Polytechnic University Pomona, USA*

## ABSTRACT

Not everyone knows what to expect when transitioning to a faculty role at a university. Mentorship is key to success in higher education. Additionally, it is important to learn the expectations for tenure and promotion while also figuring out how to manage personal and professional time. While most early career faculty members are prepared by their doctoral advisors as to what they can expect when accepting a faculty position, it is not uncommon that some essential advice gets missed. It is often assumed that junior faculty members know to write daily, and to stay on top of research but personal interests and writing time can often fall to the wayside when managing service, and teaching obligations. This chapter highlights what I feel to be my greatest accomplishment, the theories that shape by body of scholarly work, advice I wish I had received when I started in higher education, mentorship suggestions I would give an early career faculty member, and five tips for success in higher education.

*Keywords:* Graduate students; mentor; care; writing; planning

## AN ACADEMIC ACCOMPLISHMENT THAT I AM PROUD OF

One of my greatest concerns when becoming a professor was that I would struggle to teach graduate students. I had made up my mind, likely with the help of imposter syndrome, that I would not be able to successfully reach graduate students. My deepest fear was that they would see that I didn't know everything about a certain topic and that I would lose my credibility. For this reason, I would take three times the time to prepare to teach graduate courses than I would prepare for any other class. I felt that I had to have every answer. However, once I got two or three sessions into teaching my first graduate course, I relaxed and realized it was okay to say that I didn't know something. It was fortunate that the students in my first and subsequent graduate courses offered me the same grace that I offered them, necessary to the process of learning.

To my surprise, at the end of my first year of teaching, I was awarded the Outstanding Graduate Faculty Award! Each year, graduate students honor one faculty member by identifying a single faculty member who has been their most influential instructor or mentor in their education or professional development. Among the many accomplishments I have celebrated in my first 5 years as an Assistant Professor, this award is that of which I am most proud. Winning the award had not been anticipated, and it serves as a reminder that some of my greatest fears are not necessarily valid, simply because I have deemed so.

## THEORIES THAT BEST ALIGN WITH MY SCHOLARLY ACTIVITY

My scholarly activity is centered around the concept of feminist rhetorical resilience (Flynn, Sotirin, & Brady, 2012). Feminist rhetorical resilience is a concept that differs from commonplace approaches to resilience, as an individual character trait possessed by those who are able to bounce back from adversity or return to the person they were prior to experiencing adversity. Feminist resilience calls for gathering of resources and fostering relationships that present additional means to reshape possibilities, and oneself, by seizing opportunities to "change shape to meet the exigencies of…circumstances" (Flynn, Sotirin, & Brady, 2012, p. 9). I engage with feminist resilience while also working within my experiential knowledge of growing and living in the southwest Borderland. I draw from the work of Gloria Anzaldúa, and her discussions of being nepantla,

> …a Nahuatl word for the space between two bodies of water, the space between two worlds. It is a limited space, a space where you are not this or

that but where you are changing... It is very awkward, uncomfortable, and frustrating to be in that Nepantla because you are in the midst of transformation. (Borderlands/La Frontera, 1987, p. 237)

I suppose that I draw on this work as I myself am nepantla, between geographical spaces, between languages, having grown up on the border of Mexico and the United States, and much of the adversity I have experienced comes from my nepantla identities. I enact feminist resilience in response to my identities, through small gestures, relationality and sociality, as feminist rhetorical resilience calls for. I feel fortunate that I have a place to begin when I write for publications, or places from where research questions begin. My scholarly interests begin in my homes that exist in different languages, lands, and experiences. When scholarly opportunities are presented that allow me to share, or further my interest in the people's resilient responses to adversity, particularly those surrounding identity, I feel like I owe it to myself to get involved.

## HAD I ONLY KNOWN EARLIER

Having just recently spent a half hour looking at my account within the retirement website for my university, it seems that I will need to work until I am at least seventy years old. This may not be the case once I have incurred raises and hopefully will continue to contribute reasonably to my supplemental retirement. Having entered my career as an Assistant Professor at 45, retiring at 65 seems reasonable, and with good health I may not resent the need to traverse the oftentimes sprawling campus. It's not a surprise to me, that I would need to spend 25 years in this late-in-life career, in order to have a retirement on which I can live comfortably. I do have to remind myself often though, that my career is now going to span 20 or more years and I need to spend my energy with this in mind. Undergraduate, graduate, and doctoral educations are broken into workable timeframes, whereas a career in academia will be for the long haul and take me into the later years of my life.

Early in my career, I had my gears wound to short burst goals that are typical of working toward a Bachelors, Masters, and Doctoral degree. My life for eleven years was broken into parts made of a 4-, 2-, and 5-year block. Many an afternoon was spent making plans as to how I would build a Curriculum Vitae (CV) as a way of moving on to the next goal and degree. When I started my career as an Assistant Professor, I continued this way of thinking, assuming I would spend 6 years as an Assistant Professor, 6 years as an Associate Professor, and then ride out the remaining 8 or more years as a Full Professor. With this way of thinking driving my goal list, I started my career as if in a sprint, rather than a marathon. This behavior resulted in my feeling burned out by the end of my second year. I realized then that I needed to reconsider the obligations I was taking on. I also needed to revisit my goals with the knowledge that I needed to think long-term to sustain my energy.

As I begin my sixth year as an Associate Professor, I can't help but think about the first 2 years of my career. My colleagues joked in those 2 years that I should enjoy the time I had to settle into my position. Jokes swirled about the third year being the "angry year," and that my protection from being overworked would slip away in the third year. It was difficult for me to not feel insulted or resentful of my then new colleagues, feeling that I am capable of managing a number of tasks and heavy workloads. Looking back now, I see that encouragement to enjoy my first 2 years was not an underestimation of what I could do, but an urging toward what I should do. Stubborn as I am, however, I took my 3/3 course load for granted, as I did my protection from committee work and took on a number of responsibilities in my field. While I am not regretful of the decisions I made, knowing that I have met a number of wonderful people in my field as a result, I am tired. There were days in the past year that I would have agreed that I was angry, having had a chance to view the politics of the university in motion, and feeling overworked more days than not. What I wish I had known earlier in my career, however, was that this marathon of a career requires not that I see it in the same way I did my undergraduate and graduate studies, but that I pace myself while accounting for aging, the weight of responsibilities the academe places on faculty, and the need to invest free time into updating syllabi, schedules, and skill sets. Had I possessed this knowledge earlier, I would have saved some service obligations for later, been more selective about publications I strove for, and worked harder at establishing healthy routines that did not involve days filled with 10 or more hours of work.

## MENTORING ADVICE I WOULD GIVE

Success in higher education is dependent on many factors, some of which include planning, consistency, and forming mentorship relationships within one's department, field, or sphere of influence. There is a significant amount of advice given surrounding these factors, and many if not most new faculty members have reached the level of Assistant Professor because they are adept at planning, consistency, and seeking mentorship. It's less common that early career faculty members are given advice toward seeking opportunities to get involved in their field(s) through coalition and service work. While early career faculty members must be cognizant of the unpaid labor to which they become committed, coalition and conference work can provide fruitful possibilities to form relationships, to get involved in networks for sharing of resources, and to become and stay relevant regarding topics of concern to their field(s). Oftentimes, Retention, Tenure, and Promotion (RTP) requirements will include credit for service contribution within one's field. When thinking ahead toward promotion, professional organization participation is required and getting involved early in one's career can lead to leadership opportunities in the future.

## FIVE TIPS FOR SUCCESS IN HIGHER EDUCATION

I was given little advice as to how I should plan for a career in higher education. There were many suggestions as to how to complete the doctoral program and find success on the job market but beyond getting hired I felt like I had a lot to figure out on my own. The following are some tips for success in higher education that I am learning early:

1. *Develop a care plan for yourself early on that includes time to take care of your body, mind, and spirit.* This means scheduling time to move your body, feed your body healthy food, read materials that you find enjoyable, read materials that contribute to your knowledge as a professor, tend to your spiritual needs in the way that is meaningful to you, and continue or take up a creative activity that connects your body to your mind and heart. I've learned to schedule walks into my day, as well as biweekly Pilates sessions. On days when I am writing, I have learned to set my timer with reminders to get out of my chair for a 10-minute break to walk and stretch, with reminders to eat meals and snacks, and to drink water. I am faithful to lists of materials I want to read and need to read. Lastly, I schedule time in my week on Saturdays to do something creative. For me, this is paper crafts, crochet, painting, baking, and food preparation for the week ahead using new recipes.
2. *Accept responsibilities and obligations considering the real time they will take up in your schedule.* Rather than seeing a committee as a one hour per week time block on your calendar, figure the time you will need to review documents prior to the meeting, the time you will spend following up post meetings, and any invisible work that comes from taking on the responsibility or obligation. For example, I got involved with a program called Peer-to-Peer during which faculty peers visit each other's classes and offer feedback. This obligation seemed like it might take two hours per semester. I had not figured in the planning meetings as a large group, one-on-one meetings to share goals for the class, classroom plans that showcase my expertise, many exchanges of emails, and follow-up meetings.

When all was said and done, what appeared to be a two-to-four-hour obligation ended up taking close to ten hours. So, I suggest that when you take on a service obligation, you sit down with your calendar to see if you have time for preparation, emails, and mandatory meetings before accepting.

3. *Know your retention, tenure, and promotion expectations* and plan each semester according to your goals for the next step in your career. This knowledge will help you to know how many publications you need to have, the type and number of service requirements you must take on at any given time, the goals you need to aspire to in your teaching for reflection in evaluations, the amount of time you must dedicate to research, and commitments to your students, department, college, university, and the scholarly field. It's easy to over commit, or under commit if you don't think about your career as an elephant that must be eaten one bite at a time. I used to despise that saying, until I suffered too many elephant stomachaches, and remembered that Desmond Tutu knew what he was talking about, and I'd better pay closer attention.

4. *Write. Write for work, every day.* Daily academic writing will assure that you have met the publication requirements for RTP. It is important to get comfortable with prewriting, writing, and revising your research data, analysis, and newly forming research questions. With an easy-to-manage folder system on your computer's desktop, you can organize the writing you are doing and know that while one piece of writing is being proposed, another is in revision, and another is coming to life as an outline or list of notes. Write for yourself, every day. More often than not, I have to set a timer to write for myself. A habit that needs to be broken is putting my needs after the needs of others, home, and work. If only for 10 minutes a day, take time to journal, plan, create lists, and create for yourself. These are not to-do lists but lists of things you are grateful for, of places you want to see, of thoughts you had that made you laugh to yourself or smile. Journal to work out your most personal thoughts, problems, memories, and ideas. Make plans to care for yourself. Envision your Saturday, the things you will do for yourself, or the spaces that nurture you. Write a poem. Create a character, a setting, or a conflict that you can revisit.

5. *Create a plan for your semester that includes the above tips and stick to the plan,* even when your ego tells you that you can take on more, or that you would be really proud of yourself if you just took on one more possibility for accolades, recognition, or line on your CV. Remember that your ego cannot feel or anticipate the fatigue of future you. Make considerations for writing, teaching, service,

research, and most of all, care for yourself. Abiding by the plan that you created with full consideration of your goals, needs, and hopes will assure that in the future you are healthy enough to endure the demands of your career. I recommend that you sit down with the documents you've been provided for tenure, if this is the next big goal you have ahead. You can then map out short and long-term goals, estimate the number of hours attaining the goal will take, and align the hours with the hours you will spend teaching, preparing to teach, holding office hours, researching, and taking time for yourself. Time for yourself can range from time to exercise to hours spent at home when you have committed to not check email, research, or engage in class prep time. From this plan, you will be able to see how much actual time you have, and to decide which goals you want to take on each semester so that you can realistically still tend to responsibilities on and off campus.

## REFERENCES

Anzaldúa, G. E. (1987). *Borderlands/La Frontera: The new Mestiza.* Aunt Lute Books.

Flynn, E. A., Sotirin, P., & Brady, A. (Eds.). (2012). *Feminist rhetorical resilience.* University Press of Colorado.

## ADDITIONAL READING

Shadyac, T. (Director), & Tutu, D. (Political Figure). (2010). *I Am* [Film]. Flying Eye Productions.

CHAPTER 8

# BRIDGING THE GAP IN HIGHER EDUCATION: INSPIRING JOURNEYS OF WOMEN OF COLOR IN EARLY CHILDHOOD EDUCATION

Sabrina F. Hinton
*Winston-Salem State University, USA*

Saleena Frazier
*Grand Canyon University, USA*

Raleta Dawkins
*North Carolina A&T State University, USA*

### ABSTRACT

This chapter highlights the inspiring journey of three accomplished women of color who graduated from a prestigious Historically Black College and University (HBCU) and a Predominantly White Institution (PWI). The authors share their experiences as they transition from adjunct faculty to full-time educators in the Birth through Kindergarten Education department, where they found purpose and passion in early childhood education. Through their narrative, they shed light on the challenges and triumphs faced by underrepresented faculty members in higher education, emphasizing the significance of mentorship, perseverance, and the transformative power of education. Their unwavering commitment to their alma maters, HBCU and PWI, is a beacon of hope. They aspire to inspire a brighter, more inclusive future by nurturing compassionate leaders within academia. This chapter not only celebrates the strength of their journey but also underscores the immense potential that lies within every aspiring educator.

*Keywords:* Mentorship; representation; resilience; collaborations; experiences

## INTRODUCTION

As proud graduates of our esteemed Historically Black College and University (HBCU) and Predominantly White Institutions (PWI), we stepped onto the vibrant stage of academia, ready to sow inspiration in aspiring educators' hearts. The Birth through Kindergarten Education department within our exceptional HBCU became our sanctuary, where our fiery passion for early childhood education found its unyielding purpose. Our collective journey from adjunct to full-time faculty is a tapestry woven with threads of resilience, determination, and an unbreakable commitment to honor the legacy of our cherished alma maters.

As HBCU and PWI alumnae, we are intricately woven into the fabric of these institutions' storied pasts and their unwavering missions to nurture diversity, inclusivity, and excellence. We embraced the tight-knit communities and sisterhoods intrinsic to the HBCU and PWI experiences. As women of color in academia, our presence within Birth through Kindergarten Educator preparation is a testament to these institutions' dedication to amplifying representation and fostering empowerment for all.

Through the years we served as adjunct faculty members, we weathered challenges with an unwavering spirit and an unshakable belief in the transformative power of education. While we reveled in guiding and nurturing young educators, we grappled with the realities of adjunct life—contractual uncertainties and a limited grasp of benefits. Yet these hurdles fueled our resolve to conquer the odds and carve a path toward a more secure and gratifying career within the academic realm. Our journey from adjunct to full-time faculty was not solely our own; it carried the dreams and aspirations of countless budding educators who shared our stories and backgrounds. We aimed to be role models, the shatterers of stereotypes, proving that our voices and contributions were essential in shaping the future of education. As active members of academia, we strived to challenge preconceived notions and worked tirelessly to redefine the foundations of knowledge and learning. This demonstrates that a fundamental pillar of progressive education is diversity, equity, and inclusion.

Within the nurturing embrace of the Birth through Kindergarten Education department, we discovered refuge among mentors and allies who saw our potential and rejoiced in our journey as HBCU and PWI alumnae. Their constant support fortified our perseverance, reaffirming that we indeed belonged within these hallowed halls, making a profound impact on the lives of future educators.

As our narrative unfolds, we extend an invitation to walk this path with us, celebrating the unbreakable spirit of underrepresented faculty members in higher education. Our odyssey within these remarkable academic settings pays homage to the strength of persistence, mentorship guidance, and the profound influence education wields in transforming lives. With gratitude and an enduring dedication to our beloved alma maters, we embrace our roles as full-time faculty members within the Birth through Kindergarten Education department. Together, we shall continue to carry the torch of these extraordinary institutions, nurturing compassionate leaders who will illuminate a more inclusive and brilliant future. This is our story—a testament to the might of an education and the limitless potential residing within every aspiring educator.

## MILESTONES

As accomplished Black women, our journey as educational entrepreneurs has been defined by a constellation of personal triumphs and qualifications. Among these, a pinnacle achievement is surmounting the initial hesitations that often plague us and pushing forward to grasp a terminal degree. No longer constrained by the conventional climb up the corporate ladder or the maintenance of specialized expertise, we now stand tall as visionary trailblazers. Education has always ignited our passions, and we've wholeheartedly dedicated our careers to nurturing young minds within the Birth through Kindergarten Education department of this exceptional HBCU.

As Black women educators, we've been granted the honor of guiding aspiring professionals along their transformative paths toward becoming adept and compassionate educators. Witnessing their metamorphosis into confident and capable individuals swells our hearts with an immense sense of pride. The joy that blooms as we observe our students thrive in their postgraduation pursuits, leaving an indelible mark on the lives of children, is immeasurable. Each time we're privy to their achievements, it's a poignant reminder of the enduring legacy we collaboratively craft—a legacy that shapes not only the trajectory of education but also the destiny of countless children, touched by our students' steadfast devotion and ardor.

One of the most poignant and fulfilling moments in our academic journey has materialized when we received a heartfelt letter from a former student.

She attributed her academic victories to our guidance and unwavering support. Commencing her journey with self-doubt, her transformation from uncertainty to unwavering self-assuredness is a living testament to the potent impact of mentorship and educators' role in molding their students' lives. Years later, we rejoiced that she had triumphantly pursued a master's degree in Early Childhood Education, attributing our belief in her potential as the driving force that propelled her toward higher education. This experience further fuels our commitment to inspiring and empowering upcoming generations of educators, infusing them with the self-assurance and resolve needed to thrive in their chosen paths.

As we reflect upon this incredible voyage, we're struck by the weight of nurturing the distinct talents of each student and fostering a genuine sense of belonging and purpose within the academic community. As we persist in mentoring and guiding these future educators, we're humbled by the profound impact we wield as Black women educators in shaping the course of our student's lives. This realization underscores the vital significance of mentorship, encouragement, and creating an environment that nurtures curiosity and self-confidence. With deep gratitude and unwavering dedication, we embrace our roles as educators within this esteemed institution, contributing to the rich tapestry of excellence within the Birth through Kindergarten Education department and forging the path for the future of education with unwavering passion and purpose.

## THEORIES

Our journey with our former student and her remarkable transformation resonates deeply with several influential educational theories. These theories underscore the immense significance of positive teacher-student relationships and individualized mentorship. For instance, Bandura's Social Learning Theory illuminates how people learn by observing and emulating role models, underscoring educators' pivotal role as influential figures in their students' lives (Bandura, 1977). Our unwavering belief in her potential and our passion for teaching were a beacon of positivity that ignited her determination and bolstered her confidence to pursue higher education. As Bandura's theory suggests, our conduct as educators became a potent model for her, motivating her to mirror our dedication and strive for academic excellence (Bandura, 1977).

Vygotsky's Sociocultural Theory emphasizes the social and cultural context in the learning process (Vygotsky, 1978). The nurturing and supportive atmosphere within the Birth through Kindergarten Education department and our personalized mentorship cultivated a sense of belonging and purpose in our students. Following Vygotsky's theory, this environment emphasized the vital role of social interactions and collaborative learning experiences in cognitive growth (Vygotsky, 1978). In this context, the positive teacher-student relationship created a zone of proximal development, where our guidance and encouragement bridged the gap between her existing capabilities and her growth potential (Vygotsky, 1978).

These theories validate the profound influence of the teacher-student relationship on a student's evolution and accomplishments, vividly illustrating the transformative potential of education in shaping lives. By delving into and applying educational theories, educators can purposefully shape their teaching methodologies to cultivate supportive and enriching learning environments that foster academic and personal development. The narrative of our former student stands as a poignant embodiment of how these theories manifest within the classroom, reaffirming the critical importance of nurturing meaningful teacher-student interactions and personalized mentorship to empower students throughout their educational journeys.

## RETROSPECT

Understanding the transformative power of a robust professional network and the value of seeking mentorship earlier in our careers within higher education is a lesson we wish we had grasped more fully. In the fledgling phases of our academic journeys, we may have underestimated the profound impact these interconnected elements could have on propelling our success. If we had a more profound comprehension of their pivotal role, our trajectory within higher education would have undoubtedly been smoother and more impactful.

A dynamic and diverse network could have provided us with invaluable insights, guidance, and support from seasoned professionals who have adeptly navigated the intricate terrain of academia. Collaborating with peers who share our passion would have exposed us to a mosaic of perspectives, innovative ideas, and unforeseen opportunities for cross-disciplinary collaboration. Moreover, immersing ourselves within the larger academic community through a wide-reaching network would have amplified the visibility and impact of our research contributions and scholarly pursuits.

Recognizing the latent potential of interdisciplinary collaboration is another facet that could have enriched our early career experiences. Engaging in research transcending disciplinary boundaries and partnering with colleagues from various fields can open gateways to novel discoveries and breakthroughs. Such collaborations have the potential to address complex real-world challenges, attracting attention from both academia and society at large. By combining diverse expertise and viewpoints, interdisciplinary collaborations infuse the research process with fresh perspectives and innovative concepts, leading to outcomes that might not have emerged within a more isolated approach. While early career faculty members may be focused on carving their niche within their respective disciplines, embracing interdisciplinary collaborations could have unlocked enhanced visibility, increased funding opportunities, and a more profound impact on societal issues. These collaborations also foster inclusivity and camaraderie, further solidifying the sense of community within academia.

Equally important is recognizing the transformative nature of mentorship earlier in our academic journeys. Establishing relationships with experienced mentors would have provided us with a navigational compass to traverse the complexities of academia. A mentor's guidance would have directed us toward honing essential skills, clarifying career aspirations, and refining our research interests through candid feedback, constructive critique, and tailored advice. A mentor's guidance and encouragement would have alleviated feelings of isolation, offering steadfast support during times of stress and ambiguity. This bolstering of emotional well-being would have nurtured a growth-oriented mindset, empowering us to face challenges with resilience and grace.

In retrospect, understanding the potency of networking and mentorship could have redefined our early career trajectories, fostering deeper connections, amplifying our impact, and nurturing our growth as Black women scholars within higher education.

## RECOMMENDATIONS

In the dynamic landscape of higher education, we, as Black women who have traversed the academic realm, recognize the pivotal need for guidance in steering aspiring faculty members through the intricacies of their careers. Drawing from our wealth of experience and insights, we proudly present five paramount recommendations that have the potential to propel early-career faculty, particularly those who, like us, are Black women, toward a journey characterized by fulfillment and profound impact in higher education. These recommendations encompass fostering robust professional relationships, wholeheartedly embracing interdisciplinary collaborations, embarking on a continuous voyage of professional development, prioritizing the equilibrium between work and personal care, and seizing leadership and institutional involvement opportunities. By weaving these guiding principles into their academic pursuits, faculty members have the power to harness their boundless potential, make indelible contributions to their fields, and flourish as educators, researchers, and trailblazers within the academic tapestry.

1. *Nourish Solid Connections:* As black women, we understand the potency of forging authentic and supportive relationships with colleagues and mentors. Crafting a robust professional network, encompassing both kindred spirits and cross-disciplinary mentors is pivotal for navigating the labyrinth of academia. These connections not only unravel opportunities for collaborative research but also present avenues for exposure to diverse perspectives and the potential for interdisciplinary partnerships. Guiding hands of mentors, particularly those who comprehend Black women's unique challenges, can illuminate the path through academia's intricate terrain, offering sage advice, constructive critique, and the wisdom born of experience. We encourage readers to foster diverse relationships with mentors and colleagues by valuing their guidance, advocating for inclusivity, and paying it forward.
2. *Unveil the Magic of Interdisciplinary Endeavors:* Our journey tells us that interdisciplinary collaborations are fertile grounds for innovation and exploration. Merging insights with colleagues from divergent disciplines allows us to concoct new research vistas and address intricate, real-world quandaries. These partnerships knit diverse expertise and methodologies, culminating in multifaceted solutions for challenges that transcend the boundaries of any one field. Such collaborations amplify the visibility and impact of our work, and, as Black women, they enable us to bring our unique voices to the academic discourse. Reader, embrace collaboration across your field. Encourage innovative thinking, foster open communication, and value the synergy that emerges from varying perspectives.
3. *Thrive Through Lifelong Learning:* As Black women who have journeyed through academia, we understand that continuous professional development is the heartbeat of growth. Partaking in workshops, conferences, and webinars galvanizes our teaching prowess, sharpens our research acumen, and acquaints us with emerging trends. This lifelong learning showcases our unwavering commitment to excellence, enhancing our standing within academic institutions and funding circles and opening vistas of professional advancement.
4. *Nurturing the Self:* As Black women who've walked this path, we grasp the labyrinthine nature of academic pressures. While we strive for excellence, it's crucial to remember the importance of work-life equilibrium and self-care. With mindful dedication, we create boundaries, exercise regularly, embrace mindfulness practices, and indulge in activities that replenish our spirits. This commitment to well-being cements our resilience, allowing us to endure

and succeed in academia's rigorous terrain. Be empowered to take intentional time for yourself.
5. *Actively Serve:* As Black women, we recognize the potency of leadership. Our roles in academic governance, institutional committees, and curriculum design allow us to contribute to the academic community on a grander scale. These leadership ventures display our prowess and showcase our dedication to the institution's growth. They also unlock doors to greater opportunities for advancement while allowing us to make a lasting imprint on the academic tapestry.

## REFERENCES

Bandura, A. (1977). *Social learning theory.* Prentice Hall.
Vygotsky, L. S. (1978). *Mind in society: The development of higher psychological processes.* Harvard University Press.

CHAPTER 9

# SUCCESSFUL TEACHING IN HIGHER EDUCATION: HOW EXPERIENCE AS A PUBLIC-SCHOOL TEACHER, OUTDOOR EDUCATOR, AND SCHOOL COUNSELOR HELPED SET THE STAGE FOR TEACHING SUCCESS

Mark C. Gillen
*University of Wisconsin-River Falls, USA*

## ABSTRACT

This chapter outlines several important skills and training ideas to enhance the effectiveness of both new faculty members and those well into their professional careers. I discuss the importance of recognizing skills developed even before formal training. Those skills can include previous experiences and training tangential to teaching experience within graduate programs. I also discuss how to uncover teaching support once you are a faculty member, including mentoring, peer evaluations, outside training and training focused specifically on pedagogical issues.

*Keywords:* Andragogical; higher education; pedagogical strategies; experiential learning; multifaceted educator

## INTRODUCTION AND MY HISTORY IN TEACHING

Many doctoral programs provide in-depth, subject specific, training and research skill development while relegating teaching and pedagogy to a secondary pursuit. Therefore, many new faculty members begin their careers in higher education without the experience to successfully complete their instructional duties. These shortcomings are compounded when institutions provide little or no teacher training or support. This leads some faculty members to overrate their teaching skills while receiving lower ratings from students, creating issues for everyone. This chapter focuses on training and support to enhance postsecondary teaching, along with ideas that any faculty member can apply to their andragogical work.

My work as a professor really began with three early life professional experiences, Maine wilderness guide, public-school teacher, and school counselor. As a Maine wilderness guide leading groups of people on flatwater and whitewater canoe trips. Not only did I need to have the outdoor skills to survive and stay safe, but it was also essential that I train others to apply these same skills. These were not the kind of trips where the guide did all the camp work. The participants learned to do everything; using map and compass skills, improving canoeing skills, learning whitewater paddling techniques, and setting up camp with little impact on the wilderness. Additionally, I needed to live with groups of virtual strangers, engaging them at various levels while maintaining professional boundaries and expectations. I relied upon scholarship, learning outdoor skills, leadership, teaching, and practice. All vital to my future jobs.

I went from working in the wilderness to teaching fifth graders. While I did not spend 24 hours a day with my 5h-grade students, I found that as an elementary teacher responsible for all subject matters my engagement with students was like guiding wilderness trips. To enhance my teaching skills and provide supervisory guidance the school system utilized the Madeline Hunter eight-step model for mastery teaching which included anticipatory set, input, modeling, checking for understanding, guided practice, independent practice, and closure (Ramsey, 1990). This step-by-step model was not pedagogically unique but was helpful as I learned how to organize and implement educational practices in a classroom environment. Ramsey (1990) suggested that Hunter's model was useful for younger students when introducing new materials that were unfamiliar with the objective to master a knowledge or skill. Even with years of experience, and more sophisticated understanding of pedagogy, I continue to utilize parts of the Hunter model, especially when I require students to train their peers in a topic.

Like my first few years of formal teaching, the Hunter model provides graduate students an initial pathway to effective teaching.

After teaching a few years I retrained as a school counselor, worked in that role, and then moved back to experiential education and outdoor work. I took a position in a day treatment program working with 11- to 14-year-olds who were in the justice system. These were very complicated students, clients really, and I was required to engage all my teaching, outdoor and group skills. It was in the most difficult of circumstances that I finally began to focus my attention on understanding what I was doing and how I was influencing change, academically and personally, in my clients. I had to confront what was meant by success for my clients and how I applied my learning, scholarship, and training to meet their needs, and how success could be measured.

## PRIDE GOETH BEFORE A FALL: ACADEMIC ACCOMPLISHMENT

My greatest accomplishment is my continual growth with instruction. Over the last 18 years teaching graduate students, I have refined and adjusted my technique many times as I attempted to transform my instructional learning activities to engage students in supporting their own learning. For many years I successfully taught most of my courses in an engaging lecture style with experiential interactions as a side show. Lecturing when done well can stimulate student interest while maintaining their attention (Cerbin, 2018). However, as Cerbin pointed out, lecturing alone is less effective than active modes of learning. I knew from working outside of higher education that effective learning occurs when there is deep cognitive engagement with the subject materials. I had translated the action-based learning styles I had used effectively with students in higher education. I fell into the trap of teaching the way I was taught. Fortunately, my peer evaluators and students reminded me that learning is not a process where I jam all the information I know into lessons. Instead, it's a balancing act where I provide some foundational concepts and bundle them with a variety of learning opportunities, in an atmosphere often co-created by me and my students. I provide the foundation and they build upon it learning with and teaching each other as they progress.

One of the most important foundational aspects for this is relational learning, engaging in things that have meaning to them now, or can gain meaning during the process. Snijders et al. (2022) stated that a student's relationship with faculty is important but not vital. They additionally pointed out that timely responses to assignments, emails, along with interest and attention positively influenced the relationship with faculty. However, learning from peers, speakers or other professionals is also important.

On many occasions students have confronted me as to why we hadn't covered a concept presented by a peer, outside speaker, or in an article. Most of the time we had covered the topics, but like most learning the student needed to be ready to learn. And I need to be ready to help them to learn when it is the right time for them.

## THEORIES THAT BEST ALIGN WITH MY SCHOLARLY ACTIVITY

I started my educational sojourn utilizing observational theory gained by watching others teach without really knowing why they made the choices they did, followed by training in experiential learning and then Madeline Hunter's model. However, theory and practice never really connected until I began training in Solution Focused Theory (SFT) while working at the day treatment center. SFT is a counseling theory that is based on previous strength-based theories, with core beliefs that small change leads to bigger change, change is constant, and that clients oversee their change. According to Lipchik (2002) SFT is built on the foundations of the systematic paradigm. One of the goals of SFT is a collaborative connection between the client(s) and the counselor based upon a relationship building that uses purposeful listening skills to create an environment for optimum change. It is a minimalist model that emphasizes the understanding and use of theory to fully engage clients with less concern that the counselor will struggle with what to do next (Lipchik, 2002).

As an educator SFT foundational guidance helps define the balance between sharing information with students and allowing them to explore and co-create learning with myself and their peers. Having a depth of understanding about why I am doing things is more important than how to teach using specific techniques. Lipchik (2002) noted that theory is excelling in life skills, not just engaging in them. For example, she notes that good cooking is more than following a recipe, rather it requires an understanding of how different ingredients, time and temperature influence the outcome. Certainly, educators can follow a recipe for teaching, but an educational experience is enhanced when the teacher is grounded in a theory. In my case I am grounded in SFT beliefs that I apply not only in my work with students, but also my scholarship, and service to the profession.

## WHAT I WISH I KNEW EARLY IN MY CAREER

As a highly trained specialist in a field, you have a vast amount of knowledge about some things, but not everything. And almost without exception every person on your committees, and in your programs and departments are also smart people. There are always things to learn. Being confident in your knowledge and skill is important, but educational interaction is an intricate dance between teachers and learners. Each contributes to the dance, but the faculty member is less effective, and students are frustrated, if faculty do not recognize the dance the students are doing. Couple this with the vital role humility plays in all your professional work and it is easier to realize that while we may know a lot about our area, students are the specialists on themselves and their learning style.

## TWO OPPORTUNITIES TO INCREASE SUCCESS

First, I suggest faculty members seek peer feedback on their teaching. This is one of the most valuable ways I seek to improve my teaching. Probably because I was expected to participate in extensive administrative supervision and feedback early in my teaching career, I have always sought feedback in the classroom. I choose, almost exclusively, to get feedback from teacher preparation faculty. These faculty members are trained in pedagogy, it is their business. Not taking advantage of their skills and knowledge seems short-sighted. At least once a semester I invite a peer evaluator into my class. They are less familiar with the class topics allowing them to focus on how I engage student learning. I look forward to post observation discussions for the insights and ideas my peers provide as I continually evaluate my teaching and the students' learning.

Second, I think it's valuable to build on your strengths when teaching. These may include your depth of knowledge based upon your scholarship or service experience in addition to your life experience. My strengths include being comfortable with my skills and having a lifetime of experience as a counselor. I use those strengths to my advantage in preparing for classes, providing learning opportunities for students, and evaluating my class work. I teach skill-based courses integrating theory with application. I am very familiar with the material and yet each time I teach a class it is different. Students are different and learn in a variety of ways. They have different questions. They are familiar with different learning platforms. In the final analysis it is incumbent on the instructor to build a relationship with student's learning styles so they can nimbly react to issues and provide a well-conceived learning opportunity.

## MY FIVE TIPS FOR SUCCESS

1. *You Can't Read People's Minds*—Students continue to assume that I know what they are thinking, what questions they have, and the best way for them to learn. Formative and summative assignment

feedback consistently includes comments to clarify and refine basic expectations. How long does a paper need to be is a common student question. My response encourages students to take responsibility for their learning. For written assignments I provide a maximum number of pages, usually no more than two or three pages. For example, the first written assignment in their first class is a maximum of two pages, plus title and reference pages. Initially this seems like it would make the assignment simpler, however, students soon learn that writing a 2-page paper requires many more skills than writing 20 pages. Dazzle me with your brilliance, don't bamboozle me with baloney is a mantra my students often hear. I encourage students to take responsibility for their learning by reminding them that I can't read their minds, and if they have questions they need to ask, and keep asking. I do my best to respond to their questions, however, I know there may be a point where they understand, but don't like my response. Even then, we still must move on.

2. *Plan for the Worst-Hope for the Best*—I overprepare my lessons. Even lessons I have taught many times are reviewed and adjusted. During class I make brief notes to alter, reinforce, or remove material. Each group of students grasps concepts at different times. This forces me to provide the basic information clearly, and be ready with enhanced information when, and if a class requires it.

3. *Participate in On-Going Training*—In the two decades that I have been teaching in higher education there has been an epic, and sometimes overwhelming shift including on-line teaching supports and functions. Online learning platforms have eliminated the need for hard copies of papers, journals, case notes, and evaluations. The pandemic accelerated this but, training in best practice use of the learning platform is vital.

   My university requires training if you are going to teach a course fully online, but I encourage all faculty to get as much training as possible. Once you have completed the training the real work begins. Figuring out how best to use the learning platform to enhance student engagement takes time and careful evaluation. When you bundle this with peer observations, from teachers familiar with the learning platforms, your opportunities to support student learning increase exponentially.

4. *Utilize Your Teaching and Learning Centers*—Even with years of experience as an educator, and willingness to engage in peer observations, it is important to take advantage of my university's on-campus teaching and learning center staff and training opportunities. Most often used as an onboarding tool, the teaching and learning center

is most effective once faculty have experience and know what they don't know. The staff of the teaching and learning center where I have taught provided excellent, timely resources and trainings that have enhanced my skills and abilities.

5. *Take a Breath*—Not every student is going to like what you do, and they shouldn't. Students have visions of what their learning should be like. Sometimes it aligns with your andragogical style, sometimes it doesn't. Students get frustrated because learning means challenging beliefs, and learning new skills requires practice and hard work. I am more concerned if a faculty member receives perfect scores on student evaluations. After all, challenging students is vital, and that can make learning uncomfortable.

## REFERENCES

Cerbin, W. (2018). Improving student learning from lectures. *Scholarship of Teaching and Learning in Psychology*, *4*(3), 151–163. https://doi.org/10.1037/stl0000113

Lipchik, E. (2002). *Beyond techniques in solution focused theory*. Guilford Press.

Ramsey, J. G. (1990). Madeline hunter model: New faces on an old vase. *Urban Education*, *24*(4), 476–487.

Snijders, I., Wijnia, L., Dekker, H. J. J., Rikers, R. M. J. P., & Loyens, S. M. M. (2022). What is in a student-faculty relationship? A template analysis of students' positive and negative critical incidents with faculty and staff in higher education. *European Journal of Psychology of Education*, *37*(4), 1115–1139. https://doi.org/10.1007/s10212-021-00549-x

# SECTION 3

LEARN THE SYSTEM, BEAT THE SYSTEM

CHAPTER 10

# SUCCESS IN HIGHER EDUCATION: PRACTICAL TIPS FROM A LONG-TIME PROFESSOR

**Stephan E. Sargent**
*Northeastern State University, USA*

## ABSTRACT

This chapter identifies practical tips that will enable a lecturer, instructor, assistant professor, or associate professor to succeed in the tenure track. It also presents several potential "pitfalls" that may detract from success in academia. Often those entering the professoriate are highly educated, but lack the skills needed to navigate a university setting. Moreover, those who have not taught may be unsure of basic classroom teaching skills. By integrating the practical tips shared in this chapter, such a professor will benefit.

*Keywords:* Junior faculty; reading clinic; promotion; tenure; immersive learning; mentorship; collegiality; collaboration; publication; rapport

## A JOURNEY IN ACADEMIA

Becoming a successful participant in academia necessitates years of dedication, copious effort and commitment to life-long learning and continuous growth.

Such dedication to a life of service for others reaps a plethora of benefits for the new and experienced professor, alike. Having the opportunity to shape the future, continually learn, hone one's craft, and add to the knowledge of the professor's area of expertise all makes this endeavor an honor and privilege.

## ACADEMIC RELATED ACCOMPLISHMENT

Over the past 24 years in higher education, multiple universities have provided an array of excellent opportunities for me to contribute to reading/literacy education. Perhaps the greatest accomplishment which has helped the most people through the university setting has been the development, creation, and implementation of a reading clinic. When first hired at the university where I currently teach, undergraduate courses in reading methodology were taught quite traditionally using a lecture/test model. Implementation of immersive learning with a reading clinic offered the university a way to enhance the preparation of future teachers of reading (Hoffman et al., 2005) and a way to involve the community at a branch campus of the institution. The city in which the campus is located passed a bond issue, including construction of a reading clinic at the university. An executive administrator asked me to contact at least ten universities with successful reading clinics to ascertain successful aspects of their physical clinic as well as programming. Using this as a standard, the university constructed a state-of-the-art reading clinic with 20 tutoring rooms, a workroom, library, and 2 observation rooms. This magnificent facility provides tutorial assistance to students in prekindergarten through 12th grade as part of the undergraduate and graduate reading programs. Education majors now gain "real world" experience working in the clinic under the supervision of university faculty, while students from surrounding communities receive critical instruction in reading and literacy skills. The clinic's three main goals are to prevent literacy problems in the early years of school, offer a supplemental instructional program if needed and provide specialized services for those whose problems persist after intervention. The clinic provides each child with an array of assessment strategies to determine the child's needs in reading/literacy. Once the child is assigned a professional tutor, lessons are individually designed to meet the needs and interests of each child. University students directly apply content gleaned from class and are able to apply it immediately, under the tutelage of a reading/literacy professor. Not only does it assist teacher candidates to merge theory and practice, but also allows the university to reach out to the community and help real people in real time with literacy proficiency (Hoffman et al., 2005). Creation of this clinic has been exhilarating for me. First, I have the pleasure of mentoring students who have never designed or taught reading lessons. Watching candidates grow and develop over the semester is a true joy. Future and in-service teachers who have experiences in the clinic repeatedly return saying that this experience made a significant impact in how they teach children to read. Realizing how much this clinic helps teacher candidates hone their teaching skills is a delight for me. Second, I genuinely appreciate how our reading clinic provides a free service to the community. The clinical services at the university provide families with assistance in literacy that often would be inaccessible otherwise. Finding qualified assistance in literacy and affording it is a challenge for many families that the presence of our clinic ameliorates. Finally, I work collaboratively with area principals and teachers to ensure our teacher candidates have the necessary skills once they enter the classroom. This partnership ensures teachers are ready to teach reading in their classroom and makes certain that local school personnel are aware of the clinical services offered at the university. Such an endeavor has been a highlight of my academic career, leading to many pedagogical developments and scholarly opportunities.

## THEORETICAL ALIGNMENT WITHIN THE ACADEMY

While not specifically aligned with the reading/literacy field, Kolb's experiential learning theory guides my work at the university. Dating to 1984 (Kolb), this theory proports individuals learn best when proceeding through concrete experience, reflective observation, abstract conceptualization, and active experimentation. In the academy, this model guides both my pedagogical and scholarly endeavors. When teaching future educators how to teach reading, college students begin with a concrete experience. Kolb posits that "Learning is the process whereby knowledge is created through the transformation of experience" (Kolb, 1984, p. 38). In every class, from the first reading methods course, students engage in a concrete experience with a student of the age the teacher candidate wishes to teach. In each class, time is dedicated to reflective observation of the new experiences, as well as through electronic sources (such as discussion boards on Blackboard). As teacher candidates reflect on their experiences, they and others in the class share what works, disclose challenges experienced, and generate ideas for future sessions. Between class and the next clinical session, teacher candidates prepare a subsequent lesson, using ideas gleaned from reflection and modification of their initial ideas. Such abstract conceptualization emboldens the future teacher to incorporate innovative ideas into subsequent lessons. Finally, teacher candidates implement their new discoveries at the next clinical lesson, engaging in active experimentation to observe the impact of change. The process is recursive throughout the semester and leads to great enhancement of pedagogy. Overtime, teacher candidates report higher self-efficacy, score higher on state-mandated teacher tests, and perform better in the classroom as opposed to those using the traditional lecture/test model (McLeod, 2023). However, this theory not only guides my pedagogy in the classroom, but also scholarly work. My colleagues and I regularly utilize students' endeavors to conduct research. For example, a professor at another university and I are currently working collaboratively on a research project examining the efficacy of in-person versus on-line reading tutoring. Moreover, such research invigorated by Kolb's model, also allows for presentations at national conferences and subsequent publications. Kolb's experiential learning theory accentuates the importance of active participation, reflection, conceptualization, and experimentation in the learning process. This model stresses how the development of new concepts from interaction with new experiences (McLeod, 2023) well supports both the acquisition of knowledge and skills by teacher candidates and also guides the work of the professors interacting with the teacher candidates.

## I WISH I HAD KNOWN...

The retention, tenure, and promotion process in higher education, while distinctive at each institution of higher learning, is critical to the university professor. Often, at new faculty orientation, the university shares a simplistic overview of the process. However, with the demands and pressures of commencing the professoriate, placing a focus on this intricate process is easy to evade for several years. However, tenure and promotion provide job security for the professor and assist them to contribute to the field without fear of reprisal (Clay, 2018). During new faculty orientation, at one institution where I have taught, two presenters on retention, tenure, and promotion disagreed on how the process works, leaving all newly hired academics without a clear view of the procedure. Had I obtained a clear understanding from the first day of employment, much grueling work could have been avoided several years ahead.

Perhaps one piece of advice for a new professor is to thoroughly investigate the retention, tenure, and promotion process and begin on the first day of employment. Colleagues who have been through this process are well able to share their experiences, insights, and possible pitfalls. Their perspectives, as well as the information from the faculty handbook, will ensure that the efforts a new professor makes are coordinated with those who have navigated this process successfully (Duffy, 2019). As a whole, several suggestions are overarching and are applicable at any institution of higher learning. First, be sure to have and keep a curriculum vitae (CV) updated regularly. Second, be sure to save documentation for all work done. For example, save publications, attendance certificates from professional conferences, documentation of awards, records of service (for the university and profession in general), grant documentation, teaching evaluations (student and departmental), and all other documentation of related activities. In addition to saving these (hard copy or on-line), regularly organize these according to the university's guidelines. By keeping these materials up to date, a professor may easily document activities contributing to his/her eligibility for retention, tenure, and promotion (Crow et al., 2018). If one delays working with this process for several years, it may become nearly insurmountable, impacting the future of the professor's success in academia.

## ADVICE FROM A MENTOR

At the academy, a trusted mentor or confidante provides guidance/support, expertise, ideas for academic development, and increased confidence for a newly hired professor. When mentoring new faculty, I suggest two ideas for consideration. First, embrace networking at the academy through collaboration and collegiality. Developing and maintaining collegial relationships with multiple entities is exceptionally expedient at the academy (Walden, 2010). Relationships and opportunities to collaborate with administration, faculty, students, university staff, and external university supporters cannot be stressed enough. While focusing solely on classroom instruction is tempting, collaborating with multiple stakeholders develops relationships, enhances trust, improves teamwork, and supports a positive work environment. As part of collaboration with others, being visible and involved is critical. For example, serving on committees, attending events, and representing the university when needed are all examples of ways a faculty member may effectively enhance his/her initial performance at the university.

Second, maintaining a focus on scholarly efforts is critical. Again, focusing singularly on classroom teaching is enticing. However, nearly all universities (even those not labeled as R1 research institutions) value scholarly undertakings. Identifying and attending the major conferences associated with one's academic field is critical. Attendance and subsequent presentations at these conferences significantly adds to the professor's scholarly pulse at his/her institution and provides a plethora of other academic benefits. In addition, publication is crucial as well. Many opportunities exist to which a new professor may submit manuscripts. Conference proceedings, state journals, and journals within the professor's academic field all are excellent options. Although a new position in academia may seem overwhelming, these two pieces of advice will enhance a successful transition to such a responsibility.

## FIVE TIPS FOR FACULTY SUCCESS

When launching a career as a university professor, any and all recommendations may be exceedingly advantageous.

1. Seeking out the location and services of the institution's center for teaching and learning is essential. While the name of this office differs, most universities have such an entity to assist faculty. Services offered by such an office typically include assistance with pedagogy, grading, assistance with research, information/training about technology available, and many other opportunities. Faculty are experts in their respective subject areas, but often are not as familiar with pedagogical aspects required at the academy. This office regularly assists with implementation of teaching methods, student engagement, development of lectures, and use of university teaching resources. The center for teaching and learning provides a wonderful partner to help one enhance teaching effectiveness.
2. Balance work and personal time. Often the new professor is astounded by the demands immediately faced at the academy. Balancing internal demands (e.g., teaching, research, service, committees, events, university clubs, etc…) is challenging, but when coupled with responsibilities of personal life one often becomes overwhelmed. Planning time for self-care is indispensable. Spending time with family, caring for health, exercise, and pursuing hobbies all are factors associated with overall success and happiness. Some faculty actually schedule social and recreational time just as they do time for academic work and projects.
3. Learn the names of students and something about each one as soon as possible. While definitely taking work and effort (especially with online classes), this pays many dividends. Often the university has a roster available to faculty with student photos attached. Other faculty take a photo of students on the first day (some in groups of three or four to avoid large numbers of photographs) to help learn names. Others read the name of the student, look at him/her, and make a concerted effort to learn names when returning graded work. Regardless of the method, this helps build rapport and develop a connection with students. One student wrote me during the past semester noting, "You are the only professor this semester who has called me by name." Knowing that students' names are fundamental to identity, individuality, and uniqueness, this effort greatly improves the rapport established between faculty and student (Mowreader, 2023).

4. Learn to say NO! Educators often want to be all things to all people. Saying, "No," to a request may seem ill-mannered or even rude. However, learning to say, "No," to requests is critical for the new professor. Vanhouten (2015) suggests that a new faculty does not necessarily need to agree to supervise every student who asks, serve on every committee, or take on every collaborative opportunity in writing. While this may be done in a friendly, collegial manner, this practice is imperative for one in academia. First, it helps set boundaries and prioritize precious time. Also, it allows more time to utilize toward self-care and other priorities. Finally, occasionally saying, "No," to requests respects the values and priorities set by the professor.
5. Collect, utilize, and value feedback from various stakeholders at the university. Nearly all universities provide some type of course evaluations given at the end of the semester. With the advent of online evaluations, unfortunately the percentage of students participating is often low. Another excellent practice is having a trusted peer visit a class session and provide both positive and constructive feedback. I ask students each semester to provide a course reflection along with the final examination that asks them to describe two facets of the course that were useful and one item they desire to change. Dr. Julia Christensen Hughes of the University of Guelph in Canada suggests faculty utilize the "Stop, Start, Continue" technique. Using this early in the semester, students share their thoughts in each category about parts of the class they want to see stopped, started, and/or continued throughout the course (Vanhouten, 2015). Examining multiple sources of feedback is a wonderful method to help professors reflect on their practice, evaluating their pedagogical methods and impact on student learning and satisfaction.

Growth as a university professor is a life-long endeavor. Both the new and experienced academics continually learn and refine skills required for effective teaching, research, service, and positive interactions with collegiate stakeholders (Walden, 2010). While this process often seems unappreciated, daunting, and intimidating, impacting the next generation and subsequently the future of our nation makes life in the academy rewarding and recompensing.

## REFERENCES

Clay, R. (2018). Keys to success when going for tenure. *Monitor on Psychology, 49*(7), 73–84.

Crow, R., Cruz, L., Ellern, J., George, M., & White, B. (2018). Boyer in the middle: Second generation challenges to emerging scholarship. *Innovative Higher Education, 20*(1), 107–123.

Duffy, A. (2019). A delicate balance: How postsecondary education dance faculty in the United States perceive themselves negotiating responsibilities expected for tenure. *Research in Dance Education, 20*(1), 73–84.

Hoffman, J. V., Roller, C., Maloch, B., Sailors, M., Duffy, G., & Beretvas, S. (2005). Teachers' preparation to teach reading in the first three years of teaching. *Elementary School Journal, 105*(3), 267–287.

Kolb, D. A. (1984). *Experiential learning: Experience as the source of learning and development.* Prentice-Hall.

McLeod, S. (2023, June 16). Kolb's learning styles and experiential learning cycle. *Simply Psychology.* https://www.simplypsychology.org/learning-kolb.html

Mowreader, A. (2023, May 5). All in a day's work: 3 quick teaching tips for today. *Inside Higher Education.* https://www.insidehighered.com/news/student-success/academic-life/2023/05/05/all-days-work-3-quick-teaching-tips-today

Vanhouten, A. (2015, September 9). *Survival manual for new faculty.* University Affairs. https://www.universityaffairs.ca/features/feature-article/survival-manual-for-new-faculty/

Walden, R. (2010). *Tips for new faculty.* University of North Carolina Center for Faculty Excellence. https://cfe.unc.edu/wp-content/uploads/sites/326/2014/08/tips_for_new_faculty.pdf

CHAPTER 11

# THE INTERSECTION OF FINESSE AND STRATEGY: NAVIGATING THE ACADEMY AS A FACULTY OF COLOR

**Kevin L. Wright**
*Southern New Hampshire University, USA*

### ABSTRACT

Navigating academia in a Black body can sometimes reinforce the experience tied to impostor phenomena. In some cases, the experience raises the question of whether a Black scholar is viewed as a Black faculty member or a faculty member who happens to be Black and whether one is worthy in either context; both views come with a different outcome. The purpose of this chapter seeks to provide a scholarly personal narrative, along with insight and advice from an Afro-Indigenous scholar. Through this scholarly narrative, the content of the chapter provides strategies that contribute to a mission to disrupt various forms of anti-Blackness and Indigenous erasure perpetuated in formal academic settings. While discussing the three faces of power framework, an opportunity is created to further understand the nuanced experience of Black and Indigenous faculty.

*Keywords:* Faculty; Blackness; Indigenous; power; academy; intersectionality; impostor phenomena

## INTRODUCTION

This chapter will not provide all the answers to your questions. However, this text has the potential to serve as one of many resources you can use to guide your journey as a higher education faculty member. The academy is not perfect, and yet educators like you have an opportunity to add value to it alongside others that came before you. My career started in 2014 with co-instructing a first-year seminar course, and while I have accomplished so much, I still feel as if I am just getting started. In this chapter, it is my honor to share insight with you, and it is my hope that my story informs you of how you can navigate the field of higher education.

## A PROUD ACCOMPLISHMENT

One of the proudest accomplishments I have had as a faculty member was incorporating hip-hop into the curriculum of a business course. Part of the course involved discussing the foundational basics of entrepreneurship. During the course, I asked students if they were fans of hip-hop music. While all 25 students said yes, I was also made aware that their familiarity with classic hip-hop was not too strong. When I asked how many of them knew who The Notorious B.I.G. was, many of them had no idea. My response to this was layered; I was not surprised that they did not know who The Notorious B.I.G. was, however I was still disappointed. I looked at this situation as a means to both empathize and educate because I wanted the students to understand the lesson of the course, while paying homage to one of the most creative lyricists in the history of music. I had them listen to the song, "Ten Crack Commandments," and facilitated an open dialog to have them connect Biggie's lyrics to the assigned reading. I surveyed the students and asked if the reference to The Notorious B.I.G. was helpful in their understanding of foundational concepts of entrepreneurship, to which they all answered yes, as many found the assigned text of the course to be inaccessible when discussing business.

This was one of my proudest moments as a faculty member because I was able to role model in front of my students, colleagues, and supervisors how what is taught in the classroom does not have to be heavily intellectualized. Rather, it is more important to ensure the content that is being taught is accessible and relevant to students who all have different ways of learning and retaining information. From my experience, some faculty put too much dependency on a textbook or an article and expect every student to properly digest it. The classroom is a blank canvas with the students and faculty as the artists. Through this accomplishment, I was able to build pedagogical knowledge that created a transformational space where students and faculty have the opportunity to learn from each other. The importance of this experience stems from my personal upbringing and observations of others in the classroom. It was common for my peers and I to talk about the confines of the classroom as if it were a prison. We would say things like "I just gotta do my time until noon, and then I'll be free for the rest of the day," or "I got two years left before they let me out." The language we used in reference to the classroom was criminalized, and it was because of the experiences we had with educators who created such environments. When I decided I wanted to teach, I made it part of my mission to do what I can to create an environment where a student can be resourced, supported, and seen.

## SCHOLARLY ACTIVITIES

The field of academia likes to amplify a culture that upholds narratives about continuous relevancy and the publish or perish discourse. What I mean by this is that I have come across multiple educators and academic leaders stating that to succeed and thrive in the academy, you must remain academically relevant at all times. This ties into the publish or perish mindset where an educator should be publishing scholarship and research as consistently and frequently as possible and if they choose to not do so, they will not be taken seriously as faculty. Personally, I do not subscribe to either of these narratives, and I highly recommend anyone reading this text to not subscribe to them either. The reason is because this narrative is meant to justify the exploitation of the expertise, labor, and creation of knowledge among faculty who come from historically marginalized communities. Let your work speak for itself and be sure to do the things that bring you value, and that can contribute to an academically enriching experience for the students you serve.

Now if you are a person who thrives off of executing multiple studies of research and publishing various pieces of literature because you simply enjoy it, keep doing you! I have always been a writer, and my writing is led by the following questions:

- What stories and lived experiences are missing from this discussion?
- What topics either have not been researched yet or do not have enough research about it?
- What impact do I want to make with what I write?

These questions serve as my compass, which is how I have been able to partake in meaningful professional development opportunities and scholarly activities. Specifically, I have had the honor and privilege to present 25+ academic presentations at regional, national, and international conferences, along with publishing 15+ pieces of scholarship. My work has touched on topics such as cultivating a culture of philanthropy among alumnx[1] of color, men of color student retention, academic dishonesty, multiraciliaty, and disability justice, just to name a few. The beauty of having these experiences is that I get to connect and collaborate with academic leaders from all over the world, and I get to find ways to incorporate my work back into the classroom to serve students.

## WHAT I WISH I KNEW

Something I wish I knew before becoming a faculty member was the nuanced ways in which power manifests itself in the academy. A framework that explains this very well are the three faces of power (Gaventa, 2007). In this framework, the three faces of power are visible, invisible, and hidden. The visible face of power is where institutional leaders have power based on their title, and develop policies, protocols, and procedures in a particular way to control the actions of others. An example of this is when institutions have an exclusive professional dress and hair policy for faculty, or a specific expectation of how to teach and what not to say or discuss in the classroom. The hidden face of power is where a particular agenda is at play to advance a select few and disenfranchise others. An example of this is how some institutions lack transparency in terms of how certain faculty are promoted or given tenure, while others are overlooked and given nothing. Lastly, the invisible face of power is where people will accept a particular belief system as truth, and instead of challenging that belief system, they will internalize a feeling of powerlessness instead. An example is when people accept negative stereotypes about faculty of color as truth, and do not seek to mitigate or disrupt the impact of those stereotypes. I have seen the three faces of power in action too many times to count. It would have been helpful to know about situations like this in higher education prior to starting my career because my reaction would have been different. I would have been more strategic instead of combative. I will admit I burned a few bridges and approached most situations with a survival mindset.

Navigating the academy requires a bit of give and take and what I do is find ways to strategically disrupt and dismantle problematic and exclusive practices within the academy, especially if they are rooted in whiteness and white supremacy culture (Jones & Okun, 2001). An example from my experience has involved collaborating with academic executive leaders to modify policies, procedures, and protocols to be more equitable and inclusive. As an Afro-Indigenous scholar, it is my personal and ethical mission to have the academy embrace the cultural nuances of my Blackness while integrating Indigenous practices and approaches into the classroom. An example of integrating Indigenous practices into the classroom has involved reminding my peers and academic leaders about sharing power in academic environments. Specifically, I have introduced or re-introduced ways to execute various forms of pedagogy, while emphasizing that knowledge is universal, not unidirectional. This advances my purpose to decolonize higher education.

## PROFESSIONAL DEVELOPMENT OPPORTUNITIES

Two opportunities I would suggest to new faculty members are to go to conferences and to get on the good side of campus librarians. I acknowledge conferences can be expensive, overintellectualized, and extroverted-centric spaces. However, I strongly recommend new faculty members to attend conferences that cater to higher education scholar-practitioners. By going to conferences, a new faculty member has the opportunity to learn about new and thriving practices, approaches, and pedagogies that can improve their praxis and practice as an educator. Additionally, some of the toughest battles I have had to face in higher education were discussed in between sessions with colleagues at conferences. This was because conferences can sometimes provide an opportunity to have authentic and unfiltered conversations that folx would not normally have on their respective campuses.

I mentioned getting on the good side of campus librarians because many faculty underestimate how knowledgeable and resourceful they are. From personal experience, campus librarians sit on many exclusive committees, possess valuable information about research grants and scholarships, and have close relationships with administrative and executive leaders that influence the culture of the campus community. Depending on your professional interests and career aspirations, chances are the campus librarian can help you explore those aspirations rather quickly. Additionally, campus librarians have access to many academic resources that are beneficial to both faculty and students that are normally underutilized. A healthy relationship with a campus librarian is one of the strongest allies you can have on your campus.

## 5 TIPS FOR SUCCESS

1. *Don't forget your personal "why" about why you became an educator in the first place.* Sometimes, faculty forget their purpose in higher education, and usually conform to norms of whiteness. Additionally,

some faculty reach great peaks and heights in their career and forget to uplift those they pledged to serve. Each semester, take time to reflect on your personal "why" and pay attention to how it shifts over time. Let it serve as a tool to showcase the growth you experience as both a person and an educator.

2. *Create, express, and honor your personal and professional boundaries.* It can be very easy to sit on every committee, task force, and working group, but do not forget that with each extra-curricular activity you engage in, that is another environment that is taking time away from your life and is also taking unpaid labor from you as well. Find balance in enjoying your life as an educator and as a person. It is okay to say no every once in a while. Be strategic about who and what deserves access to your time, labor, and expertise. From personal experiences, I would usually say yes to every opportunity that came my way. Eventually, I reached a point where I would ask myself the following questions prior to making a commitment:

    a. Do I have the time, capacity, and energy to commit to this opportunity?
    b. Is this an opportunity that comes around frequently or rarely?
    c. What can I gain from this opportunity? What am I able to contribute to this opportunity?

3. *Network and collaborate.* Do not feel like you have to do everything alone. Furthermore, do not be afraid to ask for help. You might be surprised by how many of your peers may be experiencing similar struggles. Find your outlets of comfort and find your community of support. Pour into that community, and let that community pour into you. Networking can take place on your campus, at a neighboring institution, at a conference, or even through an exchange via e-mail. When deciding on who to network and connect with, be sure that this person has something to offer you and that you are able to reciprocate. Additionally, be sure to have a balance of people in your network who have similar and different values than you. This creates an opportunity for your network to empower you and challenge you all at the same time.

4. *Speak your truth responsibly.* To be clear, I am not advising you to stay silent, codeswitch, or be complacent; I am also not advising you to cuss someone out. Be strategic, finesse the environments you inhabit, and be sure to speak your truth in a way that is direct, respectful, and can hold others and yourself accountable.

5. *Be the reason why a student looks forward to coming back to campus.* There will be days where you may feel awesome. At the same time, there will be days where you will not feel too positive about yourself. You may experience thoughts stemming from impostor

phenomena, and you may even question your worth as an educator. However, do not lose sight of your purpose as an educator. Do not lose sight of the needs of the students you serve. You will not be perfect, and at the same time, it is crucial to finish each day where you can identify at least one thing that you consider a win.

## CONCLUSION

Like other contributing authors in this book, there is so much we could continue to discuss, and there are probably some things where we did not even scratch the surface. However, that is okay because the conversation did not start with this book, nor will it end with this book. The academy is not perfect, and yet, by having you take the time to digest the contents of this book, you are already taking a step in the right direction. As an Afro-Indigenous scholar-practitioner, there is much I have endured in both academic affairs and students affairs, and I know there will continue to be certain obstacles and struggles that I face in the future. However, I choose to not let those obstacles and struggles deter me from making a positive impact in the classroom and across campus. They do not determine my worth, they simply remind folx of my resilience. Just like the academy, I am not perfect, and at the same time, I am doing my part in reshaping it. I have the privilege to do something my ancestors did not think was possible. Proudly, I am a miracle, and a work in progress.

## NOTE

1. "Alumnx" is used intentionally to show solidarity with unrecognized individuals. I drew upon Tori Ann Porter (2016), and Danielle Torrez and Princess Reese's (2017) research who identifies the "x" to emphasize a gender binary system is a product of colonization and oppression of Indigenous Peoples. The same justification also applies to the use of "folx."

## REFERENCES

Gaventa, J. (2007). Levels, spaces, and forms of power. In F. Berenskoetter & M. J. Williams (Eds.), *Power in world politics* (pp. 204–224). Routledge.
Jones, K., & Okun, T. (2001). White supremacy culture. In *Dismantling racism: A workbook for social change groups*. ChangeWork.
Porter, T. A. (2016). *Open letter to the oppressor*. Prized Writing.
Torrez, D., & Reese, P. (2017). *Mixed-race folx*. Sutori.

CHAPTER 12

# MY JOURNEY FROM "NOTHING" TO RECEIVING AN OUTSTANDING FACULTY AWARD IN A DOZEN YEARS

**David L. Largent**
*Ball State University, USA*

## ABSTRACT

Throughout my career, I have allowed students to see that I am human, reflective, and willing to learn. The journey from graduate student to new professor, and ultimately, tenured professor may be a long and challenging path, however it can be a tremendously rewarding one. When a student gets as excited as I am about something I am teaching, I am rewarded. Every time I receive a message from a past student that says, "Thanks for helping me get to where I am today," I am rewarded. When a more experienced peer tells me they implemented something in their course they learned from me, I am rewarded. For me, the rewards have far outweighed the challenges of academia. This chapter spotlights lessons learned from parts of my journey from being a master's student, to serving as a new university professor, to receiving the university's Outstanding Faculty Award, its highest faculty award. More specifically, this chapter will highlight my experiences and share some suggestions for success that can directly be taken advantage of by faculty at any point in their career.

*Keywords:* Accomplishment; advice; cognitive learning theory; constructivism; help others; humility; opportunity; tips

## LOOK WHAT I ACCOMPLISHED, OR RATHER, WHAT MY STUDENTS ACCOMPLISHED!

Many readers may expect me to highlight one of the recognitions or awards I have received from my university and professional organizations of which I am a member. The most prestigious award I have received is the 2022 Outstanding Faculty Award, the university's highest faculty award given on an annual basis, which earned me the responsibility of delivering the university's Summer 2023 commencement address (Largent, 2023). While I am very honored and humbled to have received this award, there are dozens more faculty who are just as deserving as me—and some more so. The difference between us is not what I did, but rather what someone else did for me. I had someone who saw the good I was doing and took the time and effort to nominate me for the award.

So, if receiving the university's highest faculty award is not the accomplishment of which I am the proudest, what is?! My proudest academic-related achievement is what I have accomplished with a programming project I developed for a first-semester computer science course I started teaching during my fourth year. This course introduces foundational computer science concepts using a multimedia approach whereby learners programmatically manipulate image pixels, and sound samples, to create new and interesting media. One of the image projects requires the learner to programmatically create a collage based on multiple manipulations of a beginning image of their choosing. The resulting images are then judged by their class peers, and the best from each section of the course are displayed in a public all-section art show in a high traffic area on campus. This provides a venue in which learners can highlight their work to their peers and others, motivates learners to be creative and engaged, and increases awareness of the department within the university.

Each semester I create supporting web pages (Largent, 2025), and recruit judges (including faculty and administrators) from across the campus and externally. I create and post printed posters that contain the winners from each semester. We prominently display the two most recent semesters' posters in a high-traffic hallway of one of our academic buildings, and frame and hang older posters in a computer science classroom. The display of these posters provides local public recognition for the learners' work, and locally promotes what the department has to offer. This event has become a department tradition each semester, with the 24th show occurring last spring (at the time of this writing). My work on this project has led to multiple publications.

So why do I consider the all-section art show and its associated programming project the one academic-related accomplishment of which I am most proud? It is not because of the recognition it has brought me, although I have appreciated that. Rather, it is because of the opportunity it presents to highlight the students' work and promote the department to the wider community. Supporting and promoting others—and seeing them succeed—is a tremendous reward for me.

## THE THEORETICAL BASIS FOR MY SCHOLARLY ACTIVITY

I believe people learn best by doing and experiencing new things. This places me squarely into the cognitive learning theories school of thought, which includes theories such as constructivism, social constructivism, cognitive load theory, and pragmatic education (Drew, 2023). I draw upon all these theories, which hold that the learning process involves experiences, trial-and-error, thinking about what is observed, and making sense of it. We learn by considering our prior knowledge and thinking about how the new observed information expands or changes our prior understanding (Srivastava & Dangwal, 2017).

Social constructivism expands the traditional constructivism view to acknowledge that learning occurs while interacting with others (Drew, 2023). As an example, Vygotsky's zone of proximal development posits that learners can do some things without the help of others, they can do more things if others with more knowledge help them, and that there is a third category of things that are beyond the learner's ability at a point in time, even with the help of others. Optimal learning occurs in the middle zone (Vygotsky, 1978).

Sweller's cognitive load theory tells us that we should teach using small "chunks" of knowledge because the "working memory" of our minds can only hold a limited amount of information at a time. As such, we need to provide those small "chunks," and then allow time for it to be processed and assimilated into new knowledge (Sweller, 2011). Pragmatic education theory emphasizes that what we teach must have a practical purpose, that is, it must have utility. This is especially true for adult learners who want it to be relevant to problems they currently face in their lives (Srivastava & Dangwal, 2017).

## DON'T MISS YOUR OPPORTUNITY

The first days and months as a new faculty member are usually very hectic and overwhelming. Lots of new policies and procedures to learn, and likely some unwritten expectations that you gradually discover as time moves on.

On top of all of that, you are responsible for good teaching, getting research established, and providing service.

One thing that is easy to overlook with all the frenzy of the first few weeks and months is setting yourself up for a successful application for promotion. Granted, that process is a few years in the future, but you need to start now, so you do not need to catch up later. To be successful, you must understand what is required and expected of you for promotion—not just generically, but specifically. Find out exactly what you need to document, and how you need to document it. Ensure you understand how the promotion process works, and what you need to submit by what date.

You have likely told your students that it is more effective to do their course work throughout the semester, rather than trying to cram it all into the last couple of weeks. I am telling you the same is true for your promotion materials! Continuously document your efforts when they happen, not years later, when it is harder to remember and find the documentation you need. Doing so will make your life much less stressful when it comes time to apply for your promotion.

## DO THESE NOW FOR SUCCESS!

I have a couple pieces of advice I hope you will implement now, rather than waiting, as I have found both to be important. The sooner you do them, the more benefit you will receive. First, establish a mentor/mentee relationship. A mentor can be a great resource to help you quickly settle into academic life and its varied expectations and responsibilities. They can serve as a guide, provide advice, be a sounding board, and be an ally for you. You may find that having multiple mentors is helpful. For example, a mentor from your department may help you with department expectations, or how to teach a specific topic in a course. However, you may find having another mentor from elsewhere in your institution is helpful for topics that are not related to your department. For example, many professors in my department tend to teach in the same way. By interacting with professors who teach a totally different subject, I've expanded my "toolbox" of techniques to include approaches that I wouldn't have considered. Your academic department may have paired you with a mentor when you started your new faculty position. If so, I hope you are taking full advantage of the benefits that you can derive from that relationship. If you do not have a mentor, let your department chair know you want one, or ask someone you admire if they are willing to mentor you. And even if you have a few years of experience, having a "buddy" from whom you can explore and receive feedback can still be helpful. You will just be exploring different aspects of your academic life.

Second, establish a decent life/work balance. One of my (many) flaws is that I work too much. The problem is that I enjoy what I do, so it does not seem like work. Fortunately, I started my career in higher education after my children were adults. As such I could easily fill my time with work, rather than attending kids' activities. However, if you have children in your life, make sure you put them first. They truly do grow up too quick; you do not want to miss those experiences. Make sure there is time for you and your loved ones, as well. Habits are hard to break, especially long-standing habits. Start with a good habit of putting you and your family first.

## MY FOREMOST FIVE FOR FANTASTIC FACULTY FEATS

Many things can lead to (or away from) success for faculty in higher education. Here are five actions I have found to be important for faculty success in the academy.

1. *Be reflective and willing to change.* Be reflective about your teaching and other activities. Continuously seek more effective ways to teach and work. Question what you do, how you do it, and why you do it. Seek answers to your questions. Develop a growth mindset (Dweck, 2010). If you believe you cannot do something, rephrase that to not being able to do it *yet*. With time and effort, you will be able to. If a change is appropriate, make the change, even if it is uncomfortable. The more you do so, the more you will grow.
2. *Utilize available resources.* Take advantage of the many resources available to you. You will find resources in people, training opportunities, and classroom technology, to list a few. Always be watching for available resources. People (within your department, or elsewhere) can be a tremendous resource, providing help, tips, advice, and other supports. Your institution almost certainly offers a variety of training opportunities. These may be short one-hour events or may be multisession trainings. Participate in as many of these as your schedule will permit. Not only will you learn from the training, but you will have the opportunity to meet and interact with others from across the academy and learn from them as well. Lastly, with utilizing resources, learn how to utilize the technology that is available to you in the classroom. Learn when it is most effective to use it, and when you should not. Doing so can make you a better teacher.
3. *Collaborate with others.* Take advantage of your connections and the resources they each bring. Form collegial relationships with others, locally, regionally, nationally, and globally. Collaborate with others, even others outside of your discipline. I have been involved in

many cross-disciplinary research and writing projects, and found them rewarding, often learning new teaching and research methods because of the collaboration. Along with this collaboration, do not overlook the tremendous resources that exist in your students! Invite and encourage them to collaborate with you on your research and projects. They will bring new ways of thinking and ask questions that will help clarify what you are doing, and why you are doing it.

4. *Seek to help others succeed.* Others helped you get to where you are today, even if you are just starting your first year as a faculty member. Remember the advice and encouragement others gave you? It is now your turn to offer help to others. If you are new, you may not believe you have anything to offer, but this is not true. You have learned what works for you and have experiences to draw from. At a minimum, you can offer encouraging words to others. I am a firm believer of it being more blessed to give than receive (*Acts 20:35*, 2023).

5. *Believe in yourself but stay humble.* More than anything else, believe in yourself, but stay humble. Fight against our natural tendency to believe we do not belong in the academy. Most of us experience imposter syndrome (Feenstra et al., 2020), but know that this is normal and realize we all have doubts. You are capable, or you would not have been appointed to a faculty position. Could you improve? Certainly, we all can! Will there be times when you seriously doubt your abilities? Most likely; I still do. Realize that we all need to always be learning and improving.

At some point you will have greatly improved from those first days in your first faculty position. You may even be nominated for and awarded recognition for your accomplishments. However, do not let yourself stay up on that "pedestal," thinking you are better than others. I have found it better to be humble and always willing to learn from others—even from those who are less experienced than me. You may be surprised by how much you can learn from them.

## REFERENCES

Bible Gateway. (2025). *Acts 20:35*. Bible Gateway. https://www.biblegateway.com/passage/?search=Acts%2020%3A35&version=NIV. Accessed on July 09, 2025.

Drew, C. (2024, May 30). 31 major learning theories in education, explained! *Helpful Professor*. https://helpfulprofessor.com/learning-theories/. Accessed on July 09, 2025.

Dweck, C. S. (2010). Even geniuses work hard. *Educational Leadership, 68*(1), 16–20.

Feenstra, S., Begeny, C. T., Ryan, M. K., Rink, F. A., Stoker, J. I., & Jordan, J. (2020). Contextualizing the impostor "Syndrome". *Frontiers in Psychology, 2020*(11). https://doi.org/10.3389/fpsyg.2020.575024

Largent, D. L. (2023, July 23). Find your calling, or at least, let it find you: My commencement address. *Dave's not here, or is he?* https://davidlargent.blogspot.com/2023/07/find-your-calling.html. Accessed on July 09, 2025.

Largent, D. L. (2025, April 24). Ball State University CS 120: Computer science 1 all-section art show. https://www.cs.bsu.edu/homepages/dllargent/cs120/artShow/. Accessed on July 09, 2025.

Srivastava, S., & Dangwal, K. L. (2017). Constructivism: A paradigm to revitalize teacher education. *International Journal of Applied Research, 3*(5), 753–756. https://www.semanticscholar.org/paper/Constructivism%3A-A-paradigm-to-revitalize-teacher-Srivastava-Dangwal/57d4ecf3d7138feffeec3e8c63f184351841ede8?p2df

Sweller, J. (2011). Cognitive load theory. In J. P. Mestre & B. H. Ross (Eds.), *The psychology of learning and motivation: Cognition in education* (pp. 37–76). Elsevier Academic Press. https://doi.org/10.1016/B978-0-12-387691-1.00002-8

Vygotsky, L. S. (1978). In M. Cole, V. John-Steiner, S. Scribner, & E. Souberman (Eds.), *Mind in society: The development of higher psychological processes* [A. R. Luria, M. Lopez-Morillas, M. Cole, & J. V. Wertsch, Trans.]. Harvard University Press. (Original manuscripts [ca. 1930-1934])

CHAPTER 13

# METAMORPHOSIS OF YOUNG FACULTY: NAVIGATING ACADEMIC SELFHOOD IN HIGHER EDUCATION

**Christopher A. Hinton**
*North Carolina Agricultural and Technical State University, USA*

### ABSTRACT

This autoethnographic exposition delves into the transformative narrative of a young faculty member positioned within the pedagogical realm of a renowned R2 university in the Southeastern United States. Armed with an MBA in Human Resources and a PhD in Global Leadership the author's scholarly expedition's narrative arc unfolds, illuminating the identity establishment process within the intricate tapestry of academia. From the early challenges of securing adjunct roles to the pivotal juncture of emergent recognition, this article navigates the complex pathways of rapport-building, community cultivation, and self-navigation encountered by an emerging academic persona. Anchored within the paradigms of transformational leadership theory the narrative aligns with the archetype of the hero's journey, underscoring the faculty member's odyssey through tests of character, adversities, and the eventual conquest of scholarly prominence. The chapter seeks to elucidate the author's metamorphosis and offer insights and guidance to fellow aspirants embarking upon analogous trajectories in the academic sphere.

*Keywords:* Autoethnography; transformational; mentorship; age; lessons

## INTRODUCTION

In higher education, an emergent scholar's trajectory often weaves a tapestry that mirrors the classical hero's odyssey—a chronicle with trials, revelations, and the crucible of self-actualization (Campbell, 1949). This autoethnographic inquiry explores my voyage as a 25-year-old neophyte faculty member nestled within the academic milieu of a prestigious R1 university in the Southeastern United States. Armed with an MBA in Human Resources, my academic evolution transpired amidst a mélange of unforeseen narratives, culminating in the distinction of being the youngest faculty member in the department and the School of Business.

The genesis of my academic vacation was fraught with exigencies, as securing adjunct faculty and instructor positions proved to be a formidable pursuit. This chapter attests to the exigencies of my academic prelude and the serendipitous twist of fate that led to my current tenure. This providential juncture marked the incipience of a narrative that delves into the intricacies of cultivating connections, nurturing a sense of academic community, and maneuvering through the labyrinthine corridors of academia.

The academy is a crucible of diversity, encompassing individuals with heterogeneous backgrounds and experiences. As a faculty member with comparatively tender years, establishing rapport bore the hallmark of nuance—conversations with peers and pupils necessitating a delicately balanced synthesis of youthful dynamism and pedagogical gravitas. Fostering a sense of community emerged as a challenge, as my youth sometimes acted as a cryptic threshold, evoking an initial veil of reticence within the pantheon of my academic associates.

Amidst these difficulties, an intricate transformation process was unfurling. Anchoring within the theoretical framework of transformational leadership (Bass & Riggio, 2006), I found a conceptual lens through which to interpret my trajectory—a prism refracting the quintessential journey of the archetypal hero (Campbell, 1949). Embarking with unbridled enthusiasm and an innate thirst for intellectual maturation, the nascent faculty member embarked upon an expedition woven with trials of character, adversities, and the eventual triumph of scholarly recognition.

Subsequent sections undertake an intricate deconstruction of my transformational odyssey, articulating the stratagems, insights, and introspections that propelled me from the vestibule of ambiguity to the sanctum of academic renown (Bass & Riggio, 2006). This scholarly narrative aspires not merely to chronicle the arc of a youthful academic voyage but also to illumine a trajectory for fellow wayfarers navigating analogous peregrinations—venturing upon their academic exodus within the hallowed precincts of erudition.

## MILESTONES

A pivotal juncture within the trajectory of my academic odyssey materialized through an ascent to prominence, after being recognized as one of the most impactful faculty members within the College of Business. This distinctive acknowledgment, bestowed upon my scholarly endeavors, reverberated as a validation of my commitments and a testament to my unwavering dedication toward the revered art of pedagogy. Beyond mere accolades, this commendation resonated as substantiation for the multifarious challenges surmounted, the assiduously honed pedagogical philosophies, and the steadfast devotion invested in nurturing the cognitive growth of burgeoning intellects.

Integral to the narrative, a notable milestone that ennobled this trajectory was the cultivation of profound rapport with my students—an axis emblematic of the pedagogical essence. Manifesting as a crescendo amid the symphony of my academic voyage, this milestone epitomized the criticality of fostering authentic connections that transcend the conventional boundaries demarcating instructor-student relationships. The depth of rapport was an empirical testament to the reciprocated respect, cultivating an environment conducive to candid discourse and an unwavering commitment to the holistic advancement of each student's intellectual and personal dimensions.

However, paramount to comprehension is the recognition that these achievements are not isolated crescendos, erupting in solitude as remote pinnacles of accomplishment. Instead, they coalesce as segments of a culminating symphony, harmoniously resonating amidst a mosaic of interconnected triumphs that conjoin to shape resonant crescendos of personal and academic elevation. These accomplishments extend significance beyond discrete occurrences, each contributing a resonant note to an orchestrated composition that reverberates throughout my personal and educational maturation.

Within this symphony of interconnected victories, the thematic threads of resilience, adaptability, and an unwavering spirit resonate—catalyzing my trajectory. The symphony of my academic ascent unfurls through an intricate dance of challenges surmounted, pedagogical explorations yielding resonance, and the interplay of relationships that amalgamate into a harmonious narrative. Just as the impact of a symphony transcends crescendos to encompass delicate interludes and dynamic transitions, my academic sojourn derives enrichment from the balanced equilibrium of moments of contemplative introspection, crescendos of achievement, and transitional phases of transformative self-reflection.

Much like a symphony in which each successive note builds upon its antecedent, the interconnected victories of my academic odyssey amalgamate into a resonant crescendo of personal and intellectual ascension. My journey emerges as a testimony to the enduring ethos of scholarly inquiry, an unswerving commitment to refining the craft of pedagogy, and an innate realization that personal development harmonizes within an intricate symphony orchestrated by diverse notes that merge into complex choreography. This orchestration materializes the narrative of my academic pilgrimage as a harmonious and resonant composition—an embodiment of my dedication to scholarly pursuits, community cultivation, and the perpetual evolution of the academic self, all harmonizing with the profound artistry of cultivating profound connections with the emerging generation of scholars.

## TRANSFORMATIONAL LEADERSHIP THEORY

Within the intricate realm of academia, the trajectory of young faculty members embarking on their academic journey resembles the archetypal hero's odyssey (Campbell, 1949). As these emerging scholars navigate challenges, cultivate rapport, and seek to establish their unique identities within the academic realm, the guiding principles of transformational leadership theory offer a pertinent framework for understanding and enhancing their transformative experiences (Bass & Riggio, 2006).

Bass and Riggio posited that transformational leadership centers on the leader's capacity to inspire and motivate followers through articulating a compelling vision, fostering trust and respect, and promoting intellectual stimulation. This theory resonates with the experiences of young faculty members, who often grapple with the complexities of adapting to the academic environment, building rapport with peers, and fostering meaningful connections with students.

The transformational leadership framework can be elucidated in academic emergence through multiple facets. Firstly, articulating a compelling vision aligns with the young faculty member's pursuit of establishing their scholarly identity. Much like a leader crafting a clear vision to galvanize their team, these emerging academics must delineate their pedagogical philosophies, research aspirations, and contributions to the academic community. This articulation serves not only to clarify their objectives but also to inspire their colleagues and students by showcasing their dedication to the craft of education.

Secondly, fostering trust and respect is pivotal for young faculty members seeking to overcome potential age-related barriers and establish themselves within academic circles. The interpersonal dynamics inherent in academia often necessitate building relationships based on mutual respect and trust. Transformational leadership's emphasis on authenticity and ethical conduct resonates profoundly here, as these qualities contribute to developing rapport with peers and students, bolstering collaboration, and creating a supportive academic community (Tierney & Bensimon, 1996).

Moreover, promoting intellectual stimulation—a hallmark of transformational leadership—parallels young faculty members' challenges in cultivating a dynamic and engaging learning environment. By adopting innovative teaching methods, nurturing open dialog, and encouraging critical thinking, these emerging educators can infuse their classrooms with intellectual vibrancy, thus aligning with the ideals of transformational leadership that seek to cultivate a culture of continuous learning and growth.

As young faculty members endeavor to establish their presence within academia, they traverse a journey with tests of character, adversities, and triumphs (Campbell, 1949). This journey resonates with the transformational leadership archetype, where leaders and followers experience personal growth through challenges. The cycle of transformative leadership—idealized by Bass and Riggio (2006)—mirrors the trajectory of these young academics who evolve into influential scholars and mentors through self-reflection, resilience, and learning from their experiences.

## RECOMMENDATIONS FOR SUCCESS

The trajectory of young faculty members within the academic realm is akin to embarking on an epic odyssey—a journey laden with challenges, triumphs, and the pursuit of scholarly self-discovery. Drawing upon the insights from personal experiences, the guiding principles of transformational leadership theory, and the interplay of diverse academic nuances, this section offers recommendations to illuminate the path to success for young faculty members.

1. **Fostering Authentic Relationships:** Cultivating genuine and authentic relationships is pivotal in the complex landscape of academia. Building rapport with peers, students, and colleagues fosters a supportive academic community and engenders an environment conducive to collaboration and growth (Danaei, 2019). Embrace open communication, actively listen to diverse perspectives, and demonstrate a sincere interest in the academic journeys of others. Authenticity resonates profoundly, forging connections beyond the classroom and nurturing a sense of belonging within the academic tapestry.

2. **Seek Mentorship:** The pursuit of mentorship stands as a cornerstone for the burgeoning academic. Identifying mentors—seasoned scholars who have traversed analogous paths—provides an invaluable wellspring of guidance, insight, and wisdom (Lunsford et al., 2013). Establish a network of mentors who can give personalized counsel, offer constructive feedback, and share their experiences navigating academia's intricacies. Young faculty members should identify senior faculty that have similar background and research interests. This can be done through attending socials, networking events, and university sponsored gathering. Further, senior faculty should not be exclusive to the institution you work for; they can be identified from previous degree programs and professional organizations. Mentorship not only accelerates the learning curve but also fosters a sense of camaraderie as you forge ahead on your academic voyage.
3. **Contribute to Community:** Academic success thrives within the crucible of community engagement. Contribute actively to the academic community by participating in seminars, workshops, conferences, and collaborative projects (Tierney & Bensimon, 1996). Sharing your expertise, insights, and discoveries enriches the collective knowledge and positions you as an integral member of the academic discourse. Engage with interdisciplinary dialogs, join scholarly associations, and lend your voice to the conversations shaping your field. Further, community is crucial in feeling support as a novice faculty member, and it can be defined in many differing ways. A young faculty member should attempt to contribute to the community of their institution as well, by engaging with colleagues in their department, and throughout the campus.
4. **Celebrate Milestones and Progress:** Amidst the rigors of academia, it's vital to celebrate the milestones and progress achieved along the journey. Every publication, presentation, successful class, and positive student feedback merits recognition and celebration. These triumphs are beacons of personal and academic growth, imbuing the academic odyssey with a sense of accomplishment and motivation. Embrace the process of self-reflection, acknowledging how far you've come while setting sights on expanding your academic horizons.

In navigating the multifaceted terrain of academia, young faculty members are poised to forge their unique pathways toward success. By embracing the principles of transformational leadership theory, nurturing authentic relationships, seeking mentorship, contributing to the academic community, and celebrating milestones and progress, these emerging scholars can illuminate their academic odyssey with purpose, impact, and a legacy of scholarly excellence.

## SCHOLARLY REFLECTIONS

Retrospectively, the trajectory of my academic journey reveals a landscape adorned with indispensable lessons that have concomitantly enriched my professional and personal maturation. The journey of a developing faculty member, punctuated by encountered challenges, cultivated relationships, and attained milestones, has endowed an array of insights that reverberate as guiding principles for the ongoing continuation of this transformative expedition. Paramount among the lessons extracted from this odyssey is the omnipotent force of resilience—a testament to the unwavering fortitude that impels advancement even in the face of adversarial conditions. Every encountered setback manifested as an invitation to embrace adaptability, assimilate lessons, and emerge endowed with augmented tenacity, unveiling the intrinsic potential for growth inherent within each impediment.

A cardinal lesson materialized in the form of humility—a cornerstone requisite for pursuing scholarly eminence. Acknowledging the intrinsic necessity of receptivity to constructive critique and perpetual erudition epitomizes the cultivation of intellectual humility. An additional resounding revelation underscored the sine qua non of collaborative engagement, elucidating that the scholarly journey is inherently interwoven with the narratives of mentors, peers, and students. This cooperative dynamism enriches the academic milieu and augments the experiential tapestry of the academic pilgrimage.

Further, the significance of patient resolves emerged as a steadfast virtue, with the fruits of protracted labor often harvested across temporal dimensions. Each celebrated milestone, every forged connection, and each intellectual triumph actuates a cumulative pedagogical mosaic that embodies the didactic essence of the academic enterprise. In reverberating echoes of these lessons, the panorama of my academic odyssey attests to an enriched understanding. This illumination underscores the forthcoming trajectory with tenacity, purposeful resilience, and an insatiable yearning for the scholarly traverse ahead.

## REFERENCES

Bass, B. M., & Riggio, R. E. (2006). *Transformational leadership*. Lawrence Erlbaum.
Campbell, J. (1949). *The hero with a thousand faces*. Pantheon Books.
Danaei, K. J. (2019). Literature review of adjunct faculty. *Educational Research: Theory and Practice, 30*(2), 17–33.
Lunsford, L. G., Baker, V., Griffin, K. A., & Johnson, W. B. (2013). Mentoring: A typology of costs for higher education faculty. *Mentoring & Tutoring: Partnership in Learning, 21*(2), 126–149.
Tierney, W. G., & Bensimon, E. M. (1996). *Promotion and tenure: Community and socialization in academe*. SUNY Press.

CHAPTER 14

# THE ILLUSIVE RANK AND PROMOTION JOURNEY

**Latonia V. Moss**
*Baltimore City Community College, USA*

### ABSTRACT

The academic rank and promotion committee evaluation process typically grants professors (a general term used for all professors) an opportunity to attain this often-elusive ranking from assistant professor to full professor. In some institutions promotion includes tenure, but tenure is not necessarily a guarantee in community colleges. Nonetheless, there remains this peer evaluative process of rank and promotion that many professors have mixed emotions. An understanding of social identity theory coupled with intersectionality as the lens I used to understand the elusive process provides some reasons why the process seemed tenuous at times because of its own group membership. The author admittedly, did not understand the innuendos and writing between the lines that thwarted her initial efforts for promotion although she believed that she was qualified. This chapter offers insight into the rank and promotion process by providing strategies that helped one professor reach the rank of full professor. These strategies included active listening, growth mindset and understanding one's institutional or department's culture. This chapter seeks to share the author's personal experiences navigating the rank and promotion process along with the decision to concede the process until she gained a full understanding of what was necessary to be successful in curating a portfolio that would yield the results of her ambitions, ultimately full professor.

*Keywords:* Rank and promotion; academic success; full professor; faculty; intersectionality

## UNDERSTANDING THE PROCESS OF RANK AND PROMOTION

Historically, rank and promotion were geared to 4-year institutions where faculty were responsible for research (Orf, 2013). In 2020 there were over 800,000 full-time faculty in postsecondary institutions. Over the years there has been an increase in faculty at these institutions with 74% of full-time faculty being white men and women. Of the institutions offering rank and promotion, full professors on average made 6 figures and assistant professors averaged 70,000 a year (National Center for Education Statistics, 2023). However, community colleges differed in their roles as democracy colleges allowing open admission to students (Cohen & Brawer, 2008; Ronan, 2012). Eventually, community colleges adopted rank and promotion to "strengthen ties to higher education" (Orf, 2013, p. 12) and compete with colleges and universities for degreed faculty with at least master degrees (Cohen & Brawer, 2008; Orf, 2013) as opposed to junior college professor having a bachelor degree only. As of 2022 there were 935 public community colleges registered with the American Association of Community Colleges (Number of community colleges U.S. 2022 by type, 2023).

Hence, the Community college offered an allure for individuals seeking a career in higher education without requiring an earned doctorate degree in order to teach. Ignorant of the professorship ranks, I immediately learned that although my colleagues were called doctors or professors; professors had a ranking order. I was hired as an assistant professor and many professors who had served the institution for decades were still assistant professors. I came to understand why. Acquiring rank was this elusive process that many were denied, and others did not meet the qualifications to secure a higher rank in professorship. Nonetheless, it took me fourteen years to become a full professor. It was an uphill climb and an accomplishment worth the effort. Not only did I become a full professor, I also chaired the Rank and Promotion Committee at my institution for 2 years. This chapter will explore this elusive process and offer some strategies for faculty preparing themselves early in their career to move through the rank process.

At my institution, seven faculty members were voted to serve on the Faculty Rank and Promotion Committee, an election involving the full faculty body, and among those elected, the committee members chose a chair to lead the charge. This committee is governed by the faculty senate and reports to the vice president of academic affairs. The elected committee members serve a 2-year term. The final decision on promotion lies with the vice president of academic affairs and ultimately the president of the college who decides if funds are available to support new faculty ranks. However, it was an elected body of peers that decided who would be recommended based on their subjective interpretation of materials presented in a portfolio that qualified a faculty member for recommendation.

This recommendation culminated from a particular score that had to be reached based on a set of activities, such as professional development geared toward faculty goals and or discipline, scholarly activities, further education beyond a master's degree, students' evaluation of faculty teaching, faculty yearly evaluations, contribution to one's department and or the college community and community depending on rank sought. Although this process may differ from college to college, it is a process defined in the literature as part of rank and promotion and for most institutions, tenure in higher education (Orf, 2013). Rank and tenure can be separate or work in tandem, still most professors seek it out as an accomplishment to attain. I was no different in my attempts to seek out rank and promotion.

## UNDERSTANDING THEORY IN DEVELOPING ACTION

The theory that supported my bid for rank and promotion that helped me navigate the academic terrain was Social Identity Theory (SIT). What made SIT significant was because we are judged based on our membership in particular social groups. Whether evaluated favorably or unfavorably, our group membership effects our socialization to varying degrees (Brown, 2000; Patton et al., 2016; Stets & Burke, 2000; Trepte & Loy, 2017). Although constantly shifting between privilege and oppression, groups have their own characteristics. These characteristics can affect how individuals' social identities were explored; therefore, "social identities influence how people see themselves, how they interact with others, how they make decisions, and how they live their lives," (Patton et al., 2016, p. 67). This includes how individuals can possess healthy or unhealthy self-esteem based on the various groups in which individuals find themselves (Islam, 2014). Because SIT aided in providing an understanding of the self in higher education and society, it has proven beneficial to me in providing an understanding of the various group membership and an understanding of the intersectionality of various groups in which I am a member.

The acknowledgment of the impact of multiple identities was offered by Crenshaw (1989, 1991) who coined the term "intersectionality" as a response to women of color and the discrimination they faced and helped shape the antidiscrimination laws. Antiracist politics and Black feminine critique led to Crenshaw's (1989) concept of intersectionality. Issues of race and gender lived at the cornerstone of Black women's position in antiracist policy and feminist theory. Theoretical developments missed the mark because Black women's experiences must be reexamined to consider intersectionality (Crenshaw, 1989, 1991). Crenshaw (1991) argued that the traditional boundaries of race and gender were not incorporated into Black women's experiences. Therefore, "drawing from the strength of shared experience, women have recognized that the political demands of millions speak more powerfully than the pleas of a few isolated voices" (Crenshaw, 1991, p. 1241). An understanding that there was a collective voice among Black women even in higher education has made it easier for me to move from a place of isolation to one of a community. My experience was a part of a narrative about Black women traversing various stereotypes and using our shared experiences to encourage others.

Intersectionality was a lens that helped me understand my social identities as a Black woman and how those identities have affected me in navigating the rank and promotion terrain. SIT provided a roadmap to navigate delicate situations because of group membership whether race, gender, religion, sexual orientation, or social class, and the conflicts within each group. I have learned through SIT that although my social identity assigned me to various expectations from other groups, I learned that I was both an individual with my own ideas and a member of specific groups that may have defined me in ways that I was not. More recently, SIT expanded to include how privilege, oppression, and multiple identities effect individuals (Patton et al., 2016). A better understanding of the multidimensional facet of individuals warranted an examination into my development that was both intrapersonal and interpersonal in a social context. With SIT I was better suited to succeed in my endeavors.

## EARLY IN MY CAREER

I wish I knew how important mentoring was, but also the importance of the right mentor. It was not enough to have a mentor, but the right one. Some institutions may assign mentors (Misra et al., 2021) and that does not preclude faculty from seeking out mentors from other departments, or disciplines, or colleges. Finding mentors who will be honest in their stories and provide guidance that supported my goals was key. A mentor with an agenda that was outside of my personal agenda proved to be detrimental to my early endeavor at rank and promotion. I likened this experience to one playing God with my career. Mentors do not always know every aspect of the skills we might possess or get to decide on the timing for our promotions. Likewise, only having one mentor pigeonholed me into a particular narrative that hindered my goals. It is best to seek out mentors whose narratives are positive or neutral before linking with those mentors that negatively solidify the adage, "birds of a feather flock together." It was important to vet mentors through their involvement with others and seek the truth in what others might share about them that supports what we may suspect.

We have to be secure in our intuition. Because this adage proved true in the academy, I learned that my narrative included who I was seen with in social circles and social media posts. As challenging as building relationships and keeping networks may be, it was important for me to support my goals even when that meant distancing myself from narratives that did not support my path. Also, carefully considering what I posted on my social media pages.

## PLEASE READ THE FINE PRINT

One single piece of advice that I give to all faculty, read the Faculty Handbook. Knowing the rules of engagement at the institution I worked was paramount to my success. Knowing the rules allowed me to speak as one in authority even as a new faculty member. Also, this cued veteran faculty members that I had more than a cursory understanding of the rules of engagement, at least the written rules. Eventually, I had to learn all the unspoken rules because they existed as well. First and foremost, we have to be willing to read, and expand our bandwidth of the institution in which we work. I possessed a cursory knowledge of just about everything including the college's history. Otherwise, with more breadth and depth, I studied the policies and procedures that directly affected my success. Hence, my latter success came as a result of being a student of policies and procedures that governed the rank and promotion process at the institution where I worked. I read and marked-up documents and studied just about everything regarding the process including who had certain ranks. Additionally, it was important to read my contract each year. No matter who was the Chair, Dean, Vice President of Academic Affairs or the President of the college, my success hung on knowing what was expected of me. My stability was based on the policy and not the personality or tenure of leadership.

## WHAT I DID NOT KNOW OR UNDERSTAND ABOUT THIS ELUSIVE PROCESS

I was boldly told by a retiring colleague that I would never get promoted at the college where I worked. I was told that I did not understand the fine print of the process. The retiring colleague gave me a brief lesson on how it worked in a nutshell. The promotion committee consisted of colleagues who, despite my portfolio, often voted their subjective opinions as opposed to allowing the evidence to speak for the applicants applying for promotion. Again, as told by the retiring colleague, I was an outlier or one who walked on the margins of academic affairs. I inserted myself in student affairs and their activities that involved supporting students outside of the classroom as a means of supporting their academic performance. However,

I was warned that no one in student affairs had the ability to promote me in academic affairs. So how would I be successful in my endeavors even if I fulfilled all the requirements? None of the requirements had to do with being "liked" by the recommending seven faculty members. I centered my attention around student affairs and working in collaboration with their efforts to engage students outside of the classroom, and what I did inside the classroom to ensure retention. I could boast of maintaining 77–80% of students who enrolled in the course would be there at the end. However, I had to change and align my efforts with the group membership that possessed the power to change my rank and recommend promotion. I did, and below are five strategies that assisted me in that effort.

## FIVE STRATEGIES FOR SUCCESS I HAVE LEARNED

Success means different things to different people. Nonetheless, we can all list various things that have contributed to our success. Many aspects of moving through the rank and promotion process in higher education left me with some important strategies that I believed served me in obtaining success while growing as an educator. My list is not an exhaustive list, but meaningful and significant in ways that I hope can deliver some insights for others.

1. **Know and understand how you fit within the institutional culture:** Institutions have a culture. Departments, disciplines, and areas of an institution all have their norms too. One way to achieve success is to know and understand how one's social identity fit within the institution's culture or more closely academic affairs because that was the area where I worked. The set of assumptions that people share in the workplace is the culture that surrounds them. This was complicated by individuals' upbringings and the social and cultural contexts of institutions. Whether healthy or unhealthy organizational cultures were created by leadership and their strategic goals (Agarwal, 2018). Furthermore, leadership styles of an institution such as honest communication, teamwork, and collaboration influence the workplace environment. Although essential to our success within the academy, I learned the culture and gained an understanding of it much later in my bid for rank and promotion. It was a culture unfamiliar to the way that I worked, but I adjusted to a culture of evidence in every facet of my scholarly activities.

    My social identities did not fit squarely within the environments in which I worked. The adjustments were not painful but required much effort to make the necessary shifts to be successful in this workplace. It was an urban environment, and although I am a Black woman, my way of expressing those identities were often misunderstood because of my hair, I had dreadlocs and I was a full-figured, so a full-figured, Black women who had never been afraid of confrontation because of my individual upbringing was threatening or lacked a demure, or ultra-feminine vibe. I soften the edges and lower my voice along with understanding there was an expectation to prove my intellectual prowess. I had to not only join committees but participate in them in meaningful and visible ways that demonstrated my dedication to the field.

2. **Immediately setting goals:** It is important to know what we seek in each institution. One institution we can identify as a training ground. Another institution we can identify as a place for setting down roots. Another institution can be the place where we will retire. What I learned was that if we do not understand the academic terrain, we will set goals that do not serve our desires. Goals can guide our focus and help us sustain momentum in our careers and promote a sense of self-mastery while aligning our focus (Riopel, 2019). If a rank and promotion is a goal, it must be understood early on in our careers and where. If an institution was for training, then the goal at this institution would not be rank and promotion. We must know our end-goal, so we do not stay at one institution too long because we were afraid to move. Even set networking as a goal to meet faculty across the country to determine institutional cultures of other places we may desire to start our rank and promotion process. I am a full-professor and the only place I can go now for more income is administration, so we must know where we are going. Goals "forward" is knowing that our goals can change too (Riopel, 2019). We can move forward in our goals that have been tweaked for where we find ourselves at any given time.

3. **Controlling our narratives:** What do others think about us? It is important to have some idea of how others see us. Although we cannot control others' thoughts about us, we can mitigate negative narratives by controlling those narratives. We can be seen as curmudgeons, or we can be seen as diplomats. It is foolish to think that the power is not within our control. Not everyone will see us the same, but mitigating negative narratives and adopting positive ones is essential to thriving in the workplace. Unawareness of the unconscious script that plays in the background of our lives can often thwart our efforts (Gervais, 2020). We can change our narratives by examining the external forces that may influence how we see ourselves and how others see us. Both perceptions are essential to shaping our experiences, goals, and identities. I was

able to change what I believe was a positive aspect of myself into a better narrative after examining how what I deemed positive, others viewed as pretentious. I did not view myself in that way. I did not think I was arrogant or individualistic in nature at all. What was true was that I was an introvert who did not enjoy shallow conversation or gossip.

Hence, I had to learn how self-awareness was as much a part of controlling my narrative as gossip. We all have blind spots that can upend our efforts as a result of the lack of awareness we may possess at any given moment. Johari's window teaches us that we have four selves: open, blind, hidden, and secret (Sellnow et al., 2021). The blind self is the self others see about us that we do not realize about ourselves. With this understanding, I was able to vet what others saw and examine the narrative I was purporting. I thought long and hard about the validity of my blind spots and if there was any validity to the way others thought how I moved through the hallways. Johari's windows helped with self-awareness and as such aided me in creating a narrative that supported my bid for advancement. I could choose how to authentically exist within the academy. Authenticity was more than just being me, but understanding that I could grow into spaces that may have seemed outside of the scope of who I was. I could be comfortably authentic while growing into more.

4. **Possessing a growth mindset:** Carol Dweck and her colleagues have written widely on 'the growth mindset' (Dweck, 2015). However, what they have come to learn was that a fixed mindset was ubiquitous and simply trying to eradicate it probably promoted it further. What seemed true was that at any given time, we can possess both, and our task was to become aware of our fix-mindset way of being and intentionally choose a growth-mindset instead. A growth-mindset was more than possibilities of becoming better through effort, but adding to our efforts other strategies that demonstrated we were willing to grow. Dweck (2015) offered that we needed to live in a learning mode exploring opportunities to grow, understanding that effort alone does not constitute a growth-mindset.

Clearly, I did not change everything about myself to get promoted. There were some fixed mindsets that I was not interested in changing or putting forth any effort to address them either. I am an introvert, and I am comfortable saying, "no" to certain activities. What was important to me was to find ways to grow, which ultimately supported who I saw myself as. The authenticity of my social identities: Black, woman, Christian, and middle-class was important to me. I came to understand the complexity of my multiple social identities and the delicate dance

I had to do in order to climb the professorship ranking order. Yes, emphatically, I had to grow and grow in ways that I had not initially thought were necessary to achieve full professorship. I attended faculty events outside of the college campus. I had to join committees and participate in meaningful ways beyond my attendance. I had to lead colleagues that I normally avoided because of negativity. As with any aspiration there are necessary growing curves that we conquer in order to achieve those aspirations.

5. **Listening to intuition:** "Good listening is an essential skill in working with people" (McCashen, 2017, p. 94). Listening is a critical skill that we often dismiss its value and passively engaged with others (Sellnow et al., 2021). Active listening can be easily demonstrated in our ability to complete tasks, problem solve and validate others' experiences and perspectives (Sellnow et al., 2021). Moreover, listening allowed us to encourage civility among our peers, demonstrate care, and promote a cooperative dialog with those with whom we work (McCashen, 2017; Sellnow et al., 2021; Zenger & Folkman, 2016). Listening went beyond focused attention and nodding to denote agreement, it included feedback that increased self-esteem in others (Zenger & Folkman, 2016). I became a great listener developing interpersonal relationships with colleagues that included attending funerals, weddings, and bridal showers. Faculty were more willing to promote colleagues they knew personally in some way. Beyond our contributions no matter how great they may be to an institution; our colleagues tend to support one of their own. I knew that in theory but not so much in practice because I was comfortable in my own silo. I had to become one of them in a way that mattered to my promotion goal.

Listening included remembering names and demonstrating support and gratitude for others' contributions in committees and on projects. That was a way that listening built self-esteem in others by genuinely focusing on the positive contributions made by our peers. Negativity sometimes was expressed in ways that demonstrated hurt feelings, possible problems at home or other atrocities that faculty can experience while towing the line in the academy. Some behaviors appeared to be outside of what I deemed professional behavior or personal vendettas that seemed unfounded. But the truth was that my colleagues liken to me were dealing with personal issues and some did not know how to leave those issues home. Just setting aside time to listen to the verbal and nonverbal cues that our colleagues shout and sometimes whisper can go a long way in developing lasting congenial relationships that will support us in our efforts for rank and promotion.

## BRINGING IT ALL TOGETHER

It was with my multiple social identities, Black, woman, Christian, and middle-class background that I came to achieve the highest rank of professorship. It was not the easiest tasks to complete. There were years that I did not ever bother with the promotion process and threw the towels in and conceded the fight. There were just too many learning curves, too many innuendoes, too many personalities and too many schisms to navigate. But once I decided that I deserved to be promoted because of the work I contributed to the academy, I changed my approach to mastering the terrain. I learned the culture, set goals that aligned with the promotion process, listened, changed my narrative and I grew. I did not change who I was, I grew into this woman, this faculty member who was more astute at navigating higher education. This growth included completing a doctoral degree in community college leadership that was valuable to helping me turn a page and gaining full professorship. I gained confidence in my abilities to contribute to the work and had more compassion for those with whom I worked. I became a full professor before I was awarded the honor because I decided that I would put forth effort and incorporate strategies to obtain the desired rank.

## REFERENCES

Agarwal, P. (2018, August 29). How to create a positive workplace culture. *Forbes.* https://www.forbes.com/sites/pragyaagarwaleurope/2018/08/29/how-to-create-a-positive-work-place-culture/?sh=54468be74272

Brown, R. (2000). Social identity theory: Past achievements, current problems, and future challenges. *European Journal of Social Psychology, 30,* 745–778.

Cohen, A. M., & Brawer, F. A. (2008). *The American Community college* (5th ed.). Jossey-Bass.

Crenshaw, K. (1989). Demarginalizing the intersection of race and sex: A Black feminist critique of antidiscrimination doctrine, feminist theory and antiracist politics. *University of Chicago Legal Forum, 1989*(1), 8.

Crenshaw, K. L. (1991). Mapping the margins: Intersectionality, identity politics and violence against women of color. *Stanford Law Review, 43*(6), 1241–1299.

Dweck, C. (2015, September 22). Carol Dweck revisits the 'Growth Mindset'. *Education Week.* https://www.studentachievement.org/wp-content/uploads/Carol-Dweck-Revisits-the-Growth-Mindset.pdf

Gervais, M. (2020, March 20). Dirsupt your own narrative. *Harvard Business Review.* https://hbr.org/2020/03/disrupt-your-own-narrative

Islam, G. (2014). Social Identity Theory. In *Encyclopedia of Critical Psychology* (pp. 1781–1783). Springer. https://doi.org/10.1007/978-1-4614-5583-7_289

McCashen, W. (2017). *The strengths approach: Sharing power, building hope, creating change.* Innovative Resources.

Misra, J., Kanelee, E. S., & Mickey, E. L. (2021, March 17). *Institutional approaches to mentoring faculty colleagues.* Inside Higher Ed. https://www.insidehighered.com/advice/2021/03/18/colleges-should-develop-formal-programs-mentoring-not-leave-it-individual-faculty

National Center for Education Statistics. (2023). *Characteristics of postsecondary faculty. Condition of education.* U.S. Department of Education, Institude of Education Science. https://nces.ed.gov/programs/coe/indicator/csc/postsecondary-faculty#:~:text=Between%20fall%202009%20and%20fall,1.4%20million%20faculty%20in%202009

*Number of community colleges U.S. 2022 by type.* (2023). https://www.statista.com/statistics/421266/community-colleges-in-the-us/

Orf, M. A. (2013). *Criteria for initial appointment in rank and subsequent promotion for faculty in two-year public colleges.* Graduate Theses and Dissertation. https://scholarworks.uark.edu/cgi/viewcontent.cgi?article=1964&context=etd

Patton, L. D., Renn, K. A., Guido, F. M., & Quaye, S. J. (2016). *Student development in college: Theory, research and practice.* Jossey-Bass.

Riopel, L. (2019, June 14). The importance, benefits and value of goal setting. *Positive Psychology.* https://positivepsychology.com/benefits-goal-setting/#:~:text=Setting%20goals%20can%20help%20us,we%20truly%20want%20in%20life

Ronan, B. (2012). Community colleges and the work of democracy. *Connections,* 31–33.

Sellnow, D. D., Verdeber, K. S., & Verderber, R. F. (2021). *COMM: Speech communication.* Cengage.

Stets, J. E., & Burke, P. J. (2000). Identity theory and social identity theory. *Social Psychology Quarterly, 63*(3), 224.

Trepte, S., & Loy, L. S. (2017). Social identity theory and self-categorization theory. *The International Encyclopedia of Media Effects,* 1–13.

Zenger, J., & Folkman, J. (2016, July 14). What great listeners actually do. *Harvard Business Review.* https://hbr.org/2016/07/what-great-listeners-actually-do

## ADDITIONAL READINGS

McAlphine, L. (2016). Why might you use narrative methodology? A story about narrative. *Eesti Haridusteaduste Ajakiri, 4*(1), 32–57.

Schimanski, L. A., & Alperin, J. P. (2018, October). *The evaluation of scholarship in academic promotion and tenure process: Past, present and future.* National Library of Medicine.

www.ingramcontent.com/pod-product-compliance
Lightning Source LLC
Chambersburg PA
CBHW050539300426
44113CB00012B/2178